GEORGE WESLEY BELLOWS, Robert Henri, Frick Art Reference
Library, Collection of National Academy of Design, New York.

George Bellows
AND THE ASHCAN SCHOOL
OF PAINTING

George Bellows
and the Ashcan School of Painting

BY DONALD BRAIDER

DOUBLEDAY & COMPANY, INC.

GARDEN CITY, NEW YORK

Contents

For Susan Braider,

AN AMERICAN GIRL,

WITH MUCH PATERNAL LOVE.

I would like to acknowledge the invaluable and kindly hospitality accorded me in the research for this book by Mr. John Guido and the staff of the Library of the New York State Historical Association, Cooperstown, New York, and the friendship of the Association's Director, Dr. Louis C. Jones, and his wife, Agnes Halsey Jones, who have co-operated mightily and with whole hearts.

Introduction

From the end of the War of 1812 onward, there were two quite different stories of art in America. More properly described, one of these stories was essentially European. That is, it reflected the influence of European art on the work created here, either because the artists who were making paintings and sculptures in America had studied abroad in Paris or Rome, or because they had been swayed by teachers exposed to European tastes.

Insofar as European influences on American style and taste are concerned, there was a generation gap—as indeed there was in Europe itself. Public acceptance of Impressionism, which first made its presence *known* shortly after the end of the Civil War in the United States, did not make its presence *felt* until very nearly the end of the century. The "Barbizon" school of painting, which was a softer-lined outgrowth of a combination of earlier, conflicting factions of "Romanticism" and "Classicism" (the schools, respectively, of Delacroix and Ingres), retained its hold in both Europe and America long after the clarion call issued by the violent men of the early Impressionist group—especially the brutal Gustave Courbet and the clear-eyed realist Édouard Manet.

The word that most accurately characterizes financially and socially acceptable American and European art until the turn of the century is "politeness." It was inoffensive though skillful; for it had, in effect, been treading water for something like thirty-five years. When Impressionism began to discover a ready market in the world of major collectors, public and private, it was already being replaced by Postimpressionism and all its various forms—a development that was to announce itself in America at the celebrated New York Armory Show in 1913.

Concurrent with this Europe-oriented American art, there was a second and more interesting parade in progress, whose participants were either ignorant of contemporary European trends or had turned their backs to them—the painters of the American scene. It is too easy and very unreliable to lump this ill-assorted group under the general heading of "primitive" or "naïve" painters—for by most definitions this term suggests a lack of schooling, and by no means all the representatives of this category were lacking in formal art training. What they did have in common, with a few important exceptions (such as Edward Hicks, the Pennsylvania Quaker mystic whose visions of the "peaceable kingdom" evoke a world that never was nor will be), was a concern to depict America in its more pleasing aspects.

What these painters of our growth and customs shared with their European-influenced colleagues was a conviction that art had to be beautiful, by which they really meant "pretty"; that cartoonists might safely deal with ugliness, but not serious artists, because ugliness could not be "beautiful." They paid no heed to Keats' dictum: "Beauty is truth, truth beauty." They *had* to ignore it, because paintings of scenes that were ugly, however true to life they might be, didn't sell.

The era of American art in which George Bellows was to play an important role had its origins among a group of men who grew up and began their careers in the Philadelphia area. They were about ten years his senior. This was the period of the "Ashcan School," a name ascribed to it a decade or so after Bellows' death in 1925. How Bellows became a member of this group and, during his too-brief career, its most popular figure, is the principal subject of this book. But in order to understand Bellows and his friends, we need as well to remind ourselves occasionally of the events that were helping to shape our history and the world's—for, more than most groups of artists, the "Ashcan" painters were profoundly affected, personally and artistically, by these occurrences. They were very much the creatures of their time and circumstances. That is why art historians of today refer to these artists and their later disciples as "social realists"—because they tried to "tell it like it is."

George Bellows
AND THE ASHCAN SCHOOL
OF PAINTING

Columbus: The Early Years

Anna Smith of Sag Harbor, Long Island, was a spinster of forty when she married the widower George Bellows, architect and building contractor, and moved into the comfortable house he had constructed and long occupied in Columbus, Ohio. The year was 1880. James A. Garfield had been elected President, and the first electric street lamps were installed in New York. Andrew Carnegie saw the first steel emerge from the great new furnaces he had recently built. Lew Wallace finished writing his novel of ancient Rome, *Ben Hur,* and its publication was one of the major successes of the entire century. There were fifty thousand private telephones in the United States—but few of them were in Columbus.

If the immediate link between the old whaling village of Sag Harbor and the midwestern capital city on the Ohio River seems remote, it should be explained that the bridegroom, who was in his early fifties, had come from the East. The first Bellows to reach American shores from England had founded the Vermont town of Bellows Falls in 1632. Anna Smith's grandfather and father had been captains of whaling ships in the period when James Fenimore Cooper, better known for his novels about the American frontier, was organizing the whaling industry of Sag

Harbor into a co-operative venture that spread the profits equitably among owners, masters, and crew.

Anna and George Bellows were distantly related by blood and more closely by a common belief in the Methodist teachings of John Wesley, whose strict precepts guided their daily lives. When Anna made the move to Columbus, she brought along with her an older sister, Eleanor Smith, also a maiden lady. Eleanor, known to all her intimates as Fanny (so much so, in fact, that years later, when he painted her portrait, George Bellows misspelled her name), carried with her to Ohio a broken heart and a tale of unhappiness that was classically Victorian in its qualities of sorrow and propriety.

Fanny was in love with Sam Daggett, a married man. This state of affairs was, of course, unthinkable; but like so many states of affairs, it happened no less frequently for that—and Fanny thought about it a lot. To make the story more poignant, Sam Daggett was in love with Fanny, and he wanted to marry her. He was willing to divorce his wife, but Fanny's Methodism prohibited so easy a solution. The uniquely Victorian touch lay in the tragedy of Daggett's wife; she was incurably insane. So all that the proper lovers could do was to live apart and quietly await her death. This emphasis on Aunt Fanny's miserable life is deliberate; for her presence in the Bellows household during the childhood of the painter was crucial to his career. Had it not been for Fanny Smith, George Bellows would almost surely not have become an artist. The only other member of the family was Laura Bellows, teen-aged daughter of the master builder by his first wife.

The first and only child of this late marriage was born on August 12, 1882. He was named George Wesley Bellows, to honor not only his father but John Wesley—for it was his mother's earnest desire that her son should become a bishop of the Methodist Church. Rarely in that era, when parental wishes in such important matters were taken so seriously by children, did the aim fall so wide of the mark. For George failed to become a bishop; he also virtually renounced all religious belief.

Perhaps the cause for this spectacular defection lay partially in the atmosphere of the house in Columbus, which was almost suffocating in its fidelity to the rules laid down for daily (and especially for Sunday) conduct. To a wiry, energetic small boy, the Sabbath observance was a trial by the torture of boredom. One breakfasted early and dressed in somberest finery for church. The only relief that the little George found in the traditional Methodist service was the music—a love that developed and flourished for the rest of his life. After church came the midday meal of dinner, a repast of gigantic proportions even by the prodigal standards that prevailed in those days; for Anna Bellows and her husband were gluttonous eaters. They might be innocent of the other six deadly sins, but of gluttony, by all accounts, they were obscenely guilty. The sin was easily detected in the artist's mother. She was a very mountain of a woman.

While mother and father snoozed off the excesses of the Sunday orgy of food, their small son was dismally diverted by readings from Holy Writ or, less frequently, from high-minded classics, offered by his half sister Laura or his Aunt Fanny. At precisely what age the boy began to draw, we aren't certain, but it was probably in his fourth of fifth year. For these first awkward attempts, he used scraps of drafting paper that he found in his father's study.

What his parents made of these earliest efforts we may only surmise. They undoubtedly commended them gently, as parents are wont to praise the work of an only child. The elder George Bellows, from whom the lad *must* have acquired the talent for sketching with recognizable accuracy the objects and figures of his little world, certainly did nothing to discourage him—and nothing to encourage him, either. We find in the relationship between a boy of five and a father of nearly sixty what amounted to a two-generation gap; George's father might easily have been his grandfather. This isn't to suggest that there was any hostility between them. Rather do we find a sense of mutual bewilderment, a lack of comprehension of each other's nature—but not a want of sympathy nor any active unwillingness in either to see the other's viewpoint. The half century that separated them was a gulf that could never be bridged.

Perhaps because she so bitterly understood the loneliness that had prompted the boy to make his first scribbles, Aunt Fanny lauded them out of all proportion to their worth or skill. For it must be stated at once that the child Bellows was not, in relation to art, what the child Mozart had been to music. He had a gift, but he did not possess intuitive genius. Had it not been for his aunt's flattering support, we have every good reason to suppose that George would not have persisted in his sketching. For as he grew older he found other amusements just as attractive. So George Bellows became an artist because of Fanny Smith's enthusiasm for his boyhood work; and as we shall see, he rewarded her later on in her lonely life with material assistance and enduring affection.

When the boy was about eight, the silent Victorian tragedy that had for so long smothered his aunt's life was abruptly and happily terminated by the merciful death of Sam Daggett's wife. After a "decent interval," Daggett duly made his appearance in Columbus, married Miss Eleanor Smith who had waited so patiently, and carried her off to San Diego, where the couple enjoyed more than twenty years of matrimony before Sam died at a goodly age. With Fanny, on her departure from the Bellows house, went all the inept little drawings by her nephew; she promised to cherish them for the rest of her long life—and she did.

By the time of Fanny Daggett's marriage, George's continuing and growing interest for art was beginning to be cause for derision among his schoolmates. They were sure that any boy who actually enjoyed "art" (that word, coming from their lips, was unlikely to inspire self-confidence) was not a real boy at all. Like needlecraft and music and taffy pulling, art was for girls. Thus, in defense of his masculinity, which his friends were constantly calling into question, and unwittingly in defense of art as well, George Bellows was compelled to fight.

The opposition that he encountered at school (or more likely, on his way to and from school), combined with the indifference he enjoyed at home, probably set the seal on his determination to pursue art as a career. And he required all his nerve and all his obstinacy. Of his school days at the age of ten or a little older, when he was drawing pictures of ships that were good enough to receive the encouragement of his teachers, Bellows was later to write: "I was faced by a continual need for self-defense, and in those days either the street was too dangerous or my face and fists were wounded with the penalties of adventure." It was very good for his muscles.

It was in the summer of 1892, when he was just turning ten, that George discovered another pleasure, a passion for sports in general and for baseball in particular—and this he followed without ever thinking of abandoning his consuming desire to become an artist, a decision that his Aunt Fanny said he had made while she was still living in Columbus. There are some who would probably argue that

George became an athlete out of a need for protective coloration—to prove he could be as "regular" as any of his fellows. But this is not at all the case. His love of sport was genuine and enduring.

During the next five years, he applied to the learning of the agility and grace required by baseball the same sort of determination that enabled him to survive the mockery of his friends for his pursuit of art. Indeed, he successfully combined the two avocations by making sketches of impressive accuracy of the sand-lot ball games he watched or played in. It is curious that among highly considered artists so very few have turned their attention to baseball, for its play is as ritualized in its formality as the movements of classical ballet, to which the French painter Edgar Degas so brilliantly devoted so many works. Even the mature Bellows made only an occasional sketch or lithograph of baseball themes.

By the age of fifteen, the gangling George, who had very nearly attained his maximum height of six feet, two inches, was a regular outfielder for the local sand-lot team and for the varsity team of Central High School, a building designed and constructed by his father, which he entered in the autumn of 1897. He was neither a very good nor a very bad student. He got by reasonably well with only token effort in most subjects. With the exception of geometry (an interest that would later prove useful to him as an artist), his concerns were chiefly extracurricular—baseball, basketball, and glee club. He also made all the illustrations for the school's monthly paper.

The drawings he made at this time were shameless imitations of the illustrations of Charles Dana Gibson, the high priest of illustrative art at the turn of the century, the creator of the richly contoured Gibson Girl, the ideal

American man's ideal American woman. George contributed drawings to publicize a high school revue in the fall of 1900, shortly after the presidential election that had seen William McKinley of Cleveland returned to office, with the former Governor of New York and hero of the disgraceful Spanish-American War, Theodore Roosevelt, as Vice-President. George caricatured these two public figures and also the features of McKinley's right-hand man, Mark Hanna, also of Cleveland, who many considered to be the most important person in Washington, the principal presidential adviser. But there was certainly nothing disrespectful in George's portrayals of these celebrities. If he held any political opinions with conviction at this time, they were undoubtedly those with which he had been brought up. The boy's father thought McKinley a great Chief Executive, particularly in comparison with the Democrat, Grover Cleveland, who had preceded him. If the elder Bellows had any reservations about Teddy Roosevelt, they were with regard to what many considered his radical views on conservation and such matters as child labor. However, Roosevelt had been selected to run with McKinley to put him out of the way. Though just a heartbeat away from the presidency, the Vice-President was powerless, and this was just what his enemies wanted.

The last winter of the nineteenth century saw George cast in the part of basketball star. His height and his agility were great assets. But his activity on the Central High School baseball team was impressive enough to provoke the offer of a tryout with the Indianapolis club of the Western League. According to those who saw him play in 1901 and later gave evidence of his prowess, George was a first-class glove man, an admirable base runner, but of poorish talent at the plate. The offer, whatever it consisted of, wasn't tempting enough to prevent the young athlete from continuing his education. Besides, his true vocation remained art, and he had the satisfaction of graduating from Central High with the prediction from his art teacher that he had a great future in the field he had chosen for himself.

Columbus: University Days

George Bellows entered Ohio State University in his native Columbus just a few days after the death of President McKinley, in September 1901. The unthinkable had happened. An anarchist, Leon Czolgosz, had shot him on the sixth; on the fourteenth, McKinley had expired. Theodore Roosevelt was President. The reaction in Columbus was probably one of greater shock than in other parts of the country, because McKinley had been an Ohioan. But consternation was general. McKinley had not been a great head of state, but the apprehension inspired by his assassination was justified. Something, almost everybody said, must be done to stop the spread of anarchism—a movement that had first shown its power in America during the Haymarket Riots of Chicago in 1886. A law was duly passed by Congress prohibiting the entry into the country of any foreign anarchists—but of course, as the President was among the first to point out, there were plenty here already, more than plenty.

We have no information about George Bellows' personal response to this dramatic and tragic event. One must presume, however, that he sympathized with the general feeling that no matter how admirable the causes the anarchists claimed they were serving, violence was not the suitable means of advancing them. This was certainly his position a few years later, when he himself became remotely involved in the hottest issue of the hour; but a few years later he was better-informed. In the fall of 1901, he probably agreed with almost the entire nation that the anarchist movement was a clear and present danger to the country. The difficulty confronting the agents of justice at this time and for a whole generation to come lay in distinguishing between the philosophical anarchists and the active anarchists. It was a distinction few policemen thought it necessary to make. And in 1901, it was doubtless a distinction that George Bellows, who knew nothing about anarchism except what he might have read in the press, didn't even know existed. For him, as for practically everyone else, the anarchists were the 1901 equivalent of the hippies, yippies, peaceniks, and student activists generally —with a strong foreign element, mainly Slavic. His ideas would gradually change, but this change didn't take place in Columbus, Ohio.

George had divided his summers, before entering the university, between work and play. At his father's insistence, he had already learned every aspect of the building trades during a succession of summer vacations. These talents, twenty years or so later, would serve him in good stead. This holiday following his graduation from high school was no different. He worked on a construction site, and he played baseball. Toward the middle of August, he joined his family on a trip to Sag Harbor. The return journey was broken by a short visit to the Methodist camping ground of Lakeside, on Lake Erie, where all things were meant to be bright and beautiful for the soul because they were so dismally uncomfortable for the flesh.

Because he continued to live at home, college didn't represent much of an emotional transition for George. Ohio State was merely an extension of Central High School. But there was also his quite astonishing temperament, which made it possible for him to adjust easily to almost any change in circumstance. Long accustomed to being a non-conformist and to accepting whatever social or even physical penalties this kind of eccentric behavior incurred, he found himself readily accepted at Ohio State for what he was; here, his various qualities were more happily and more immediately recognized than they had been at Central High.

A measure of George's courage and strength of conviction was his attitude toward ROTC, mandatory at Ohio State, as it was at all land-grant colleges and universities at that time. He had a quiet genius for making a virtue of necessity. So did he despise the required ROTC participation that he decided to avoid it. He learned to play the drums, became a member of the band; by the following summer, he was so good a drummer that his services were in demand for band concerts. His approach to almost every experience throughout his life was affirmative.

His academic interests were not much more consuming than they had been in high school. The single exception was English, as taught by Professor Joseph Taylor, who happened also to be an amateur water-colorist and who was drawn at first to George by art rather than literature. The student responded by manifesting a new and exciting curiosity for the English language, particularly for the poetry of Walt Whitman (which many Americans thought scandalous), and the controversial plays of the Irishman George Bernard Shaw, whose political and social ideas were considered extremely radical in a nation whose domestic policy was "every man for himself," whose foreign policy traveled under the name of "dollar diplomacy," and that greeted its thousands of immigrants each year as "the wretched refuse" of Europe. Certainly the frequent visits to Joe Taylor's house during the student's years at Ohio State prepared his mind for the intellectual changes that were to show themselves later, and established a friendship that endured for the rest of the artist's life.

The freshman athlete's skill and height afforded him a place on the Ohio State basketball squad that winter; but though he was a much better shortstop than the senior playing that position on the varsity baseball team in the spring of 1902, he was unable to get a regular berth. The coach's high opinion of him, however, was confirmed the next summer when he asked George to play in the infield on a semi-professional team he managed in Columbus.

In the fall of his second year at Ohio State, George enrolled in his first formal course in art: "color standards, color theory, color harmony, color appearance, tone and gradation," he later wrote of it, "illustrated with lantern slides." He did additional work on his own initiative in the area of water colors, with the advice and encouragement of Joe Taylor, who soon was compelled cheerfully to acknowledge that the student was far more proficient than the master.

George also studied economics, a subject that, as offered at Ohio State, was so straightforward a defense of *laissez-faire* capitalism that it was to have, eventually, the effect of turning the artist into a socialist—though at this point in his life he merely accepted the conservative doctrine as it was preached, for it left him in total ignorance of any alternative system of economic or political thought. George Bellows was not the last student to be forcibly directed toward radicalism by the rigidity of his elders' way of life and thought.

His attractive, rapidly made sketches had already brought him to the attention of the editors of the Ohio State year-book, who made ample use of his work. In his sophomore year, he found an additional outlet (and source of funds) in the yearbook of Kenyon College. All the drawings he made were extremely derivative, in the taste of the era, of the illustrations of Charles Dana Gibson, whose work he had been imitating for a long time, and of Howard Chandler Christy and John Singer Sargent—the latter just coming into his own as the most fashionable of American portrait painters.

From our vantage point of nearly three quarters of a century, we may be astonished to note that George found the time and energy to be the star of the basketball team and, the following spring, the first-string shortstop, in addition to his studies and his semi-professional work in art. (The regular baseball team that year, incidentally, included seven players from the group with whom George had played at Central High School.) He also joined a fraternity and took an active part in that diverting aspect of university life. The explanation for so much and so widely varied activity lies partly, of course, in George Bellows himself, who was never happy if he couldn't get enough physical exercise—and for him, enough exercise was usually more by far than the average man would think reasonable. It lies as well in the easy tempo of college existence, which was far less demanding intellectually than is the case today. Moreover, even at such hallowed institutions as Harvard, it was considered ungentlemanly to excel in one's studies. Getting by was the thing. George got by.

The summer of 1903 produced two circumstances that deeply affected George Bellows. Over the first, a wave of lynchings in the South that were unprecedented in their savagery, he had no control. Yet the vivid descriptions in the local papers remained forever in his mind and, like the course in economics he had taken the previous year, were to help in the permanent formation of his political and social outlook. It would be too much to say that he had become a liberal in his philosophy; but everything he encountered was pushing him in that direction—unintentionally. The second circumstance was of his own making. For the first time, he and his aging father collided head on over the question of George's future. Although this initial difference of opinion ended inconclusively, it was fateful; for the son recognized that he would, sooner or later, be compelled to force the issue. His father would never voluntarily consent to George's choice of art as a profession.

The third year at Ohio State was, in its general outline, much like the first two. He played basketball and baseball; he made all the drawings for the university yearbook; he studied the art and architecture of ancient Greece. The only major novelty was a course in jurisprudence that appears to have left no mark on him at all. The major event of his junior year had neither intellectual nor artistic implications. It occurred in the spring, when he was scouted by a representative of the Cincinnati Reds and received an offer to try out as shortstop. Since he rejected the suggestion, we cannot know what the outcome would have been. He must, however, have been an extraordinarily deft infielder, because his height worked against him. Had he become a major-league shortstop, he would have been taller than any other player to occupy that crucial spot except the great Marty Marion of the Cardinals. By the end of his third year of college, George Bellows had two distinctions: he was the only American destined to become a successful artist who had refused to become either a bishop or a professional infielder.

Through the academic year, the running argument at home continued over his future. His half sister Laura and her husband, Ben Monett, strongly sided with George in the struggle with his father. Anna Bellows wanted peace in the house at almost any price, for by now she appreciated that her religious aspirations for her son were groundless. At the conclusion of the spring term, George reached a critical decision. He wouldn't take any of his final examinations. This would rule out the possibility of his being accepted at Ohio State the next autumn as a senior. (Dropping out, in 1904, didn't have the implications it has today. A small percentage of the population possessed bachelor's degrees, so the B.A. didn't constitute an essential license for seeking "dignified" employment, as it does now.) Presented by this *fait accompli,* George's father lost his resolve. If the son hadn't convinced him, he had at least spiked his guns.

George spent the summer in Columbus accumulating as much money as possible for his projected move in the autumn to New York—because, as he had so frequently and fruitlessly explained to his father, New York was the only city in America where he could further his education in art. If this assertion wasn't an absolute truth, it was nearly so. Philadelphia and Boston did have their academies of fine arts, but the great market place was New York.

To enrich himself as best he could, George employed his two best talents: he played semi-pro baseball, and he made sketches for the Columbus newspapers. By the end of August, he had amassed the not inconsiderable sum of five hundred dollars. We don't know just what George Bellows the younger said to George Bellows the elder at this vital moment of his life, but it must have been very persuasive. For the old man, so irrevocably opposed for so many years to his son's plans, suddenly relented. He promised to send him fifty dollars per month for expenses as long as the money was needed. It is a wise man who knows better than to try to fly in the face of nature.

George and his father parted sorrowfully but amiably. Neither ever gave the other reason to regret the decision. To the end, they remained friendly, even though the differences of age and viewpoint made it impossible for them to be friends.

New York: Years of Discovery

George Bellows had passed through New York with his family on the journey to and from Sag Harbor, but he had paused there only briefly. To live in the city was to enter the world. And the world of 1904 was not the happy planet that many people (the ones who speak fondly of "the good old days") like to imagine. There were wars in Africa and in the Far East. There was oppression everywhere. There was poverty and a great disparity between the rich and the poor. There was violence in the South, where the whites were trying to put the blacks back "in their place" after nearly forty years of post-Civil War Reconstruction, and in labor-management relations—the strike as a weapon in the struggle for improvement of wages and working conditions didn't enjoy great popularity. Teddy Roosevelt had recently broken a five-month coal strike by threatening to work the mines with troops. The first legislation regulating the use of child labor had passed through a not very eager Congress only a year before. About 40 per cent of all industrial capital was in the hands of the "trusts," whose interlocking directorates gave them immense political as well as economic power. Teddy Roosevelt, seeking re-election to the presidency against the opposition of Judge Alton B. Parker, whose Democratic Party was sundered over the question of paper currency, could boast that he had struck a major blow against the trusts in the celebrated *Northern Securities* case, and that he had negotiated a treaty giving the United States the right to build the Panama Canal.

New York is a lonely city if you have neither friends nor relatives living there. But under the same conditions, so is Columbus, Ohio. George Bellows, aged twenty-two, knew no one on his arrival in the largest American city in September 1904. He did, however, have two advantages, in addition to his small income, not granted to everyone going there to seek education or fortune or fame: He knew precisely what he wanted to do, and he was an exceptionally outgoing and easygoing young soul. He made friends without difficulty, and had no trouble keeping them. There is no record of a broken friendship in his entire life—an achievement that few can truthfully claim.

Just after the turn of the twentieth century, New York was not quite so overwhelming a place as it is today. There were few automobiles. Most of the trolleys were drawn by horses. The subway, from City Hall to upper Manhattan, had just opened. The trains of the several elevated railways were steam powered. The Queensborough Bridge was under construction. The Manhattan Bridge had not yet been undertaken. Pennsylvania Station, today replaced by the third structure to bear the name Madison Square Garden, was no more than a sparkle in the eye of Colonel Robert Cassatt, president of the Pennsylvania Railroad and father of Miss Mary Cassatt, one of the few American painters of her period to develop, within the broad framework of revolutionary French concepts of art, her own technique and outlook. Mary Cassatt, however, was in Paris, and George Bellows thought himself fortunate to be in New York.

As it is today, the city in 1904 was difficult to describe,

but less so, because it was smaller and more manageable. *The* skyscraper was the "Flatiron" Building, which dominated Madison Square. It was the hub of Manhattan. Another triangular structure, the Times Tower, was rising at the intersection of Broadway and Forty-second Street. The two edifices were the architectural sensations of the day.

To a far greater degree than now, New York (and in fact the whole establishment of American political, economic, and social life) was effectively governed by White Anglo-Saxon Protestants, the "WASPS," who have only recently and belatedly been accused of most of our present domestic and foreign troubles. Theirs were the money, the power, and the glory. They occupied most important political offices and all the important social ones. They determined tastes and tried to determine morals (although, as even now, they threw up their share of eccentrics). Morals, however, had nothing to do with the way they earned and kept their money, for money had no morality; money was power, and power was a prize for which men eagerly killed one another—as today.

The social structure of the city (and the nation) was a lot more rigid than it is now. The rich were very rich because such taxes as were levied hardly affected their income or capital. The rich formed the upper level of society by embracing, through marriage or simple proximity, the handful of families who had managed to keep their great holdings in land and thus more or less to justify their claim to be "aristocrats." It was the epoch of the "robber barons," as the writer Matthew Josephson called them—the Harrimans, Rockefellers, Morgans, Carnegies, Mellons, Vanderbilts, Goulds, Fricks, Flaglers, and Havemeyers, of families who had risen to dazzling financial heights by emptying the purses of the more scrupulous and/or less fortunate.

New York was endowed with a very distinct middle class
—merchants, professional men, educators—many of whom
undoubtedly aspired to the incalculable riches of the "Four
Hundred," a term coined in this era to denote the exclusivity of "acceptable" society. The middle class and
the rich lived just around the corner from each other,
from Washington Square north to Fifty-seventh Street along
Fifth Avenue, or on the lower stretch of Riverside Drive.
The former occupied the side streets, the latter the avenues—
Fifth Avenue being by far the "best" address, with Madison
Avenue running a very safe second.

Most numerous and most easily distinguished and iso-
lated were the poor. They were mainly crammed into the
Lower East Side of Manhattan, from which they occasionally
contrived to escape by saving enough from their pitiful earnings—but far more often by dying, which they did in ap-
palling numbers. Their living conditions, and especially those
of the immigrants who arrived in great quantities until the
onset of World War I in 1914, had been vividly described
by the Danish-born journalist Jacob Riis in *How the Other
Half Lives*, a book that appeared in 1890 and caused
dismay to the privileged, who preferred to pretend, as many
still do, that the culture of poverty is "picturesque" and that
the poor live as they do because they like to.

This New York of 1904 has been described at such
length because, from the very beginning of his life in
Manhattan, George Bellows became, in a variety of ways,
a true creature of the city. More than any other artist of
his generation, he was obsessed by all aspects of metropolitan existence. He prowled every street from the Battery
north to Riverside Drive. During the next twenty years, he
would portray the city in all its opulence and squalor, its
high life and low.

Artists have always occupied a strange and unique corner of every society, dependent for their livelihood on the whims of the rich and (consequently) attached to their culture, after a fashion—yet also intellectually and culturally separate from them. Such was the circumstance in New York when George Bellows arrived. The city's artistic activity was controlled (though, as we shall see, not very effectively governed) by the National Academy of Design, a self-perpetuating club that counted among its members very few renegades—because renegades were rarely successful artists and because only successful, recognized artists were admitted to the Academy. It was a vicious circle. The National Academy of Design was what we would call today the "Establishment" of contemporary art, and because its members thought very much alike on the subjects of painting and sculpture, they didn't think very much, and certainly didn't approve of artists who would dream of rocking the boat whose tranquil voyage they wanted to enjoy without interruption or annoyance.

But annoyance was at hand, and quite unwittingly George Bellows fell in, from his very first days in New York, with the group of artists who would provide most of the disturbance. After settling into respectable but much too confining quarters at the YMCA on Fifty-seventh Street, he immediately presented himself for admission to the New York School of Art, a block or two west on the same street. This institution was owned and operated by a distinguished and successful member of the National Academy of Design, William Merritt Chase, and was known as the Chase School. A portraitist of some renown, Chase greatly admired the expatriate James Whistler (dead only a year) and preferred to clothe himself in the curiously formal attire he had selected for the portrait Whistler had made of him.

Since art students weren't so numerous as they are

today, and since many of them hadn't the money to pay
their fees, Bellows (with money) had no difficulty in
gaining a place in Chase's school. It was as simple as the
folklore about being inducted into military service; one
had only to be warm. Chase welcomed the young man from
Columbus and immediately placed him in the charge of
Robert Henri, his most popular teacher.

How remarkable a figure Henri was, almost no one of
his own time really knew. Only a recent biography (*Robert
Henri and His Circle*, by William Innes Homer) has revealed the painter's past. The son of a Mississippi riverboat
gambler whose later career involved unsavory real estate
dealings and, finally, murder, Henri's real name was Robert
Henry Cozad. To avoid disgrace, the artist dropped his
last name and, out of acknowledgment of French blood
that flowed in his veins, adopted the Gallic spelling of his
middle name, which he pronounced "*Hen*-rye."

Henri went to Philadelphia, where he began his art studies at the Pennsylvania Academy of Art. There he formed
friendships with a number of his contemporaries, notably
John Sloan, William Glackens, George Luks, and Everett
Shinn, all of whom came eventually to New York to
practice and/or teach. These five painters represented the
nucleus of a group that would finally be called "The Eight,"
rebels all against the heavy, authoritarian hand of the
National Academy of Design.

About ten years older than Bellows, Henri had followed
the time-honored tradition of studying in Paris; there
he had fallen under the influence of Édouard Manet, the
true father of the revolution in painting that we now know
as Impressionism. However, it was Henri's most significant
conviction about the teaching of art that he should seek
to bring out in each of his pupils that which was individual,
unique—the person's own instincts and tendencies. Of Henri,

who became a lifelong intimate, Bellows was to say that he was the single most important figure in his artistic development—for the very reason that Henri helped him to discover himself.

Their first meeting showed the direction their relationship would take and the nature of Henri as an instructor. When Bellows presented himself for his first class period, Henri immediately asked to be shown the work that George had been doing in Columbus. After studying the sketches the young man had brought along, most of them cartoons for the Ohio State yearbook, and all of them (as we have already observed) owing almost everything to the styles of the day's popular illustrators, Henri inquired blandly, "Haven't I seen these before?" The deflated pupil wordlessly returned the drawings to his portfolio and never referred to them again.

Henri's great message, insofar as the philosophy of art was concerned, was that any subject was the suitable property of the artist. "Draw your material from the life around you, from all of it. There is beauty in everything if it looks beautiful to *your* eyes. You can find it anywhere, everywhere." It was advice that George Bellows was to follow with much greater fidelity than did the master who proffered it.

As colleagues at the New York School of Art, the new arrival from Ohio numbered several young men who would achieve celebrity, especially Edward Hopper and Rockwell Kent, whose diverse talents as artists were to be widely and properly recognized, and Clifton Webb, whom William Merritt Chase had the perceptiveness to push in the direction of the stage, where, he rightly believed, Webb's true genius lay. Another student was Edward Keefe of New London, Connecticut, whose father (like George's) was an architect who (like George's) had been very reluctant to see his son turn to the economic uncertainties of a career in art when offered the solid possibilities of the construction business. Keefe was to try his hand as an art student for a limited time (unstipulated); if, after a sufficient period had elapsed, the young man felt he had real promise, his father would continue to support his efforts. If not, Keefe was to return to New London and become an architect. It was a fair arrangement and a wise one, proving that fathers are not invariably mistaken.

With Ed Keefe and an acquaintance from Columbus, Fred Cornell (who had come to New York to find romance and adventure in the employ of Western Union), George Bellows rented rooms in West Fifty-eighth Street, just around the corner from the Chase School. The quarters were hardly spacious enough to accommodate the easels of two painters, in addition to beds and other furnishings for three—but they managed cheerfully through the months of winter and spring.

With the closing of school for the summer, Keefe went back to New London and Cornell to Columbus, leaving George to his own devices. To eke out his savings and his meager allowance, he had been earning a few dollars weekly as a member of the choir of the Broadway Tabernacle. To this, with the onset of the warmer weather, he now added semi-pro baseball, which was played on diamonds in Central Park—just a block north of his rooming house. At other times, and especially during the long twilights of the summer months, he wandered about the city with Henri's words in his mind that beauty was to be found anywhere and everywhere. The result of these strolls was his first independently conceived oil painting, which he called *Night Scene;* it is interesting to us mainly for its intimations of Bellows' work to come.

When September arrived and the Chase School reopened,

Robert Henri was still enjoying himself, with his wife and some students, in Spain. His classes were temporarily taken over by a friend and fellow graduate of the Pennsylvania Academy, John Sloan. Sloan had supported himself for some time by designing "fancy goods," candy boxes, Valentines, and similar items, for A. Edward Newton, who would later achieve a certain renown as a collector of rare books and writer on that subject. Sloan and Henri saw eye to eye in the matter of artistic philosophy. Sloan's etchings (of which he was a master) reflect his convictions to a far greater degree than do Henri's paintings. And the approaches of the two men to instruction could hardly have been more different. Where Henri was affable and patient, Sloan was embittered and irascible; where Henri was constructive, Sloan was gruff and scornful.

Sloan had to fill in for his associate for only a few weeks, but in that period Bellows (who liked almost everyone) developed a fondness for the man that was reciprocated—to the best of Sloan's ability. In spite of the differences in age and temperament, the two became friends. On his return, Henri expressed pleasant surprise at the progress George had made during the summer holidays. He at once asked the young Ohioan to visit him at home, and George soon became a regular participant in the informal gatherings at Henri's house every Tuesday evening. So, just a bit more than a year after his arrival on the scene, George had a foot in the first of a number of doors he would have to open in order to attain complete recognition. The Henris were the most cordial of hosts to the select group invited to their house. It consisted almost entirely of painters—the men who would be called "The Eight"— the five graduates of the Pennsylvania Academy together with Arthur B. Davies, Ernest Lawson, and Maurice Prendergast.

These artists, wrote the art historian Peyton Boswell, Jr., were " . . . a confraternity of men of common interests who hung together, much like a group of American newspapermen in a foreign capital. Glackens and Lawson were 'painting America' as impressionists; Davies, as a poet; Sloan as a direct-on-the-spot reporter. As a unit, they set the stage for things that were to come; they gave direction and spiritual leadership to native art other than that offered by the [National] Academy [of Design]."

Of "The Eight" Henri alone had the distinction of being a member of the Academy that represented the enemy to all of them. He was, as well, a director of the Society of American Artists and Sculptors, a group that was soon to be merged with the older Academy—though this combination was not effected without a great deal of verbal bloodshed. The academicians viewed with infinite disdain and active hostility any kind of art whose virtues were not immediately discernible as those preached by their members. Consequently, annual exhibitions sponsored by this august institution only rarely featured paintings or sculptures that violated the rules of good taste that the juries of the Academy knew by heart (and by purse). But where else could the art of rebellious or aspiring young artists be seen?

This very question was posed without satisfactory answer at virtually every Tuesday evening gathering in Robert Henri's house. Artistic rebellion was in the air, but as yet, no one was quite certain how it would reveal itself or from what quarter the first trumpet call would come. This unhappiness over the state of the arts was a corner of a more generalized unhappiness about the state of the American union. Along with many other groups of thinking citizens, Henri and his friends were most fretful about the complacency of the majority of Americans in the face of what seemed to be a number of burning issues—the most significant of which appeared to be whether or not labor should be free to organize and to bargain collectively. The division among the intellectuals of 1905 was not so much over the relative merits of capitalism and socialism as over those of socialism as opposed to anarchism.

Anarchism, the rejection of the very idea of central government, came in two distinct flavors—political and philosophical. The political anarchists espoused violence. The philosophical anarchists deplored violence, but deplored with equal fervor the violent methods used to suppress the activities of the political anarchists. If the reader detects a strong similarity between the problems and debates of our own day and those of 1905, he would not be much in error. The specific issues were different, but the principles involved are extraordinarily alike. What was then regarded as one of the main benefits of the socialist state in its ideal form—economic, political, and social justice—has by now long been accepted by both of our major political parties as very respectable public policy. But the application of that policy to all our citizens has yet to be achieved, and the arguments heard in 1905 are astoundingly familiar to Americans of 1970: Can this policy best be implemented by peaceful or by violent means? The political anarchists of 1905 advocated and practiced a program of force and terror that would find many harmonies with the principles and actions of contemporary political activists. The end, they said, justified the means.

Just where George Bellows first stood in these heated disputes it is difficult to say with certainty. Like many an American of our own day, he was undoubtedly torn between the experience of his upbringing in the ultraconservative atmosphere of the Ohio state capital and the humanitarian impulses of his nature. As a guest of Henri's, he was probably presumed to be a socialist, and very likely an atheist as well—ideas that would have devastated his Methodist-Republican parents in Columbus. But we may reasonably guess that his walks through the city's streets the previous summer, seeing just how in fact the other half lived, had a profound influence on his future political thought. It's entirely probable, as a matter of fact, that Bellows had seen more of the slums than most of Henri's friends—excepting, perhaps, Sloan and Glackens.

There was another tendency in the young artist that would affect his outlook: his true sportsman's sense of fair play. No one who had patrolled for any length of time the poverty-stricken portions of New York could say with conviction that the teeming masses huddled there actually enjoyed their conditions—a strange argument which, as we have remarked, was prevalent among a high proportion of the more fortunate. So it was that George Bellows (whether gradually or suddenly) became a socialist with distinct sympathies for the position of the anarchists. As we shall see, his political viewpoint was to form an essential base and basis for his art.

But political conversations, whether about the politics of the nation or that of the small, insular world of art in New York, were in this second year of study a comparatively minor matter in the life of Bellows. His painting came first, and as Henri's most promising pupil, he flourished in his chosen line of work. In the course of this academic year he painted portraits of his friends Ed Keefe and Clifton Webb. And he fell in love.

The modern reader may well wonder that no mention of interest in girls has cropped up in the Bellows story until now. The reason is that there is no surviving record of any profound attachment during the Columbus years. So we must presume that there was none. The object of his first and enduring affection was a former student of the New York School of Art, Emma Louise Story, two years his junior. He had noticed Emma from time to time the year before but had certainly not perceived in her what he detected when, wholly by chance, he met her while she was making a rare visit to the school in October. Thus began a romance and courtship that must make the strongest mortal weep over its duration, its exasperations, its postponements, its frustrations. Yet of such things is made the perverse deliciousness of love. George adored Emma from their first meeting, and this put him at a disadvantage of which she was well aware; he continued to adore her, though she trifled with him mercilessly and heartlessly for nearly five years.

If George Bellows was a young man of his time, so Emma Story was a young woman of hers. The second daughter of a lace and linen merchant whose business was steadily declining, she had moved with her parents first from expensive New York to the less costly but rather fashionable suburb of Montclair, New Jersey, and then, when trade faltered even more, to the less prosperous community of Upper Montclair. The Storys were early disciples of Mary Baker Eddy's Christian Science, a faith to which Emma adhered without bigotry. Her older sister had, in addition, embraced the vigorous feminist stand of Lucy Stone, and to this new creed of full equality for women in all things, Emma also subscribed, though again without prejudice.

She was handsome, not quite beautiful (but almost), with fine white skin, clear, candid eyes, and splendidly abundant dark hair. She liked art, as evidenced by her attendance the previous year at the Chase School. But she had renounced it for the study of music, which interested her more. She was a pianist of solid, though not brilliant, accomplishment. On the whole, if these alone were Emma Story's best qualities, it seems doubtful that she could for so long have commanded George Bellows' undivided attention and adoration. What appears to have been her greatest appeal to him was her remoteness, her inaccessibility, her reserve, her refusal to take him very seriously—though she well realized how very serious were his feelings for her. He wanted her all the more because she so infrequently gave him even a semblance of wanting *him*. She liked him—nothing more, and nothing less, either. She tantalized him in this way for years, good-naturedly, but never in cold blood. It was her nature to be diffident. As the folk saying has it, Emma ran from George until she caught him.

They "walked out" together often in the autumn and early winter evenings, discovering many common interests. Most of all, they enjoyed each other's company, sharing especially a love of laughter and its obverse, a healthy delight in argument. They quarreled often about almost everything—even things they were in fundamental agreement over. While both were in the process of intellectual and spiritual emancipation from the shackles that had bound them from childhood to their parents' habits of thought, each viewed this new freedom from a different angle. Their disputes were as lively and wholehearted as their outbursts of gaiety.

When Emma learned that George couldn't afford to return to Columbus for the Christmas vacation, she invited him to Upper Montclair, where, for the first time, he met her mother and father. William E. Story and the very tall, very reedy young art student made a strange pair. There was absolutely nothing for them to talk about. Story professed to a total ignorance of art, though he claimed a nodding acquaintance with the American painter George Inness, of whom Bellows knew little and cared less. Emma's father had no interest in sports, not even in baseball, which seemed to Bellows almost un-American. There remained the topic of textile manufacture and merchandising. But William Story could converse only about linen, and George could talk only about canvas. Yet, good sense and good temper prevailed against apparently hopeless odds. George and the man who would eventually become his father-in-law got on as well as they needed to.

Fortunately for Bellows and for art, his love for Emma didn't very often obscure his work and study. Early in the new year, shortly before the sudden death of Robert Henri's wife, he painted a picture that disclosed a second aspect of his deep concern for popular pursuits of the poorest city dwellers. It was a recollection of a scene he had repeatedly observed the preceding summer in New York that he called *Forty-two Kids;* it represented a swarm of naked boys swimming off a pier on the East River.

At the urging of the widowed but resilient Robert Henri, George exhibited this painting the next March at the annual show of the Society of American Artists, where it caused something of a scandal—not because of the nudity of the children but because of the "crudity" of the subject matter. The same accusation was leveled against Sloan and Glackens, though more temperately. Not since the long-forgotten years of William Sidney Mount, an artist who had flourished more than a half century earlier, had a professional American painter seriously turned his hand to "popular" subject matter. But Mount had depicted rural scenes; Bellows found his inspiration in the ugliness of the city. It was not done, the critics smugly complained. Yet Bellows was doing it. If he was still far from being a success, George now possessed a name that was known, and that was a lot more than could have been said at the beginning of the year 1906. He sensed that he was making progress, even if he couldn't prove it by the sale of his work.

In June, Bellows took Emma on a ferry ride to Staten Island. There, he assured her, the view of the late spring moon was much better than any to be found in Manhattan. Evidently carried away by the lunar beauty and the nearness of the girl of his dreams, he became more affectionate than she thought proper, and she lost no time in telling him so in a manner well calculated to humiliate him. They parted abruptly on this unfortunate note, and for two interminable days Emma allowed her suitor to suffer the anguish of what he supposed to be permanent rejection. Then she relented, and wrote him an amiable letter excusing his transgression and promising never to refer to it again. She kept her word about forgiveness, but until their marriage, four years later, Emma made frequent and very owlish allusions to George's love of the moonlight, especially as seen from Staten Island. He took the teasing well—because it came from her.

In July, Emma departed with her parents for a holiday in Nova Scotia, where she dallied with a young doctor and took ferocious joy in writing to George of the attentions this luckless fellow, doubtless as smitten with her as the painter was, insisted on showing her. In sweltering New York, there was only moderate consolation for Bellows in the scandal that rocked the city—the murder of the prominent architect Stanford White by millionaire Harry K. Thaw. White had offended his killer by taking as his mistress Thaw's wife, a former showgirl whose favors had been liberally granted to other distinguished New Yorkers. The only cultural legacy of this sordid business was a rash of jokes; all described the wronged husband entering a

newly erected building and, smiting his forehead, mutter-
ing, "My God, I shot the wrong architect."

George's parents passed through New York in the middle of July on their way to Sag Harbor. History doesn't
relate what they thought of his rather squalid living conditions, but there was no suggestion, so far as we know, that
he renounce his life for a return to architecture and construction in Columbus. They invited him to join them on
eastern Long Island, and he eagerly accepted. Before making the excursion, however, he completed a portrait of an
urchin of his Fifty-eighth Street neighborhood, Thomas
McGlannigan, a picture he called *The Cross-eyed Boy*,
and a number of small paintings depicting New York life
in summer—the best-remembered being *River Rats*, a var-
iant of *Forty-two Kids*. He also made a single attempt
at etching, hoping through the sale of prints to duplicate
the success in this field that John Sloan was enjoying. But
he discovered immediately that the delicate, meticulous
technique of engraving adapted itself poorly to his sweeping, vigorous style. He never tried to etch again.

A fortnight or so at Sag Harbor was welcome relief
from the heat and confusion of the city. But it is vital
to an understanding of George Bellows' character to temper
this observation with another; as a rule, he was happy
wherever he found himself, as long as there were companionship and the opportunity for physical exercise. He seems
never to have much relished solitude, even when he
was working—though occasionally in later life he did com-
plain that there was a bit too much noise in the house to
permit him to concentrate. It would be difficult to imagine
an artist more easygoing, sensible, extroverted, and friendly
than Bellows, at least as far as the world was concerned.
Only one illustrious parallel comes at once to mind—that of
Peter Paul Rubens, the great Flemish painter of the seven-

teenth century whose nature was as sunny and whose response to life was as affirmative as Bellows'. Neither should be offended by the comparison.

When his two weeks at Sag Harbor had passed, George happily returned to New York, to semi-pro baseball in Central Park, to his painting and sketching, and to plans for a removal to more spacious surroundings. He had located what he considered an ideal setting for work and living, an immense studio on the sixth floor of the Lincoln Arcade Building at 1947 Broadway. In September, he was joined there by Ed Keefe, coming back for another year of study with Chase, and Fred Cornell, who arrived again from Columbus.

It was soon clear that no matter how highly George thought of these new quarters, the opinion was not enthusiastically shared by Mr. and Mrs. William Story, who called one afternoon with Emma not long after the young artist had moved in. Seeing Bellows for the first time in his native habitat, so to speak, Emma's father suddenly failed to understand what his daughter could see in this raffish young Bohemian who chose to live what had the appearance of an extremely irregular life in highly unusual surroundings. It may be, too, that on the occasion of this visit George and Story discovered a common interest—politics, and that from this discovery evolved a discussion that revealed their extreme differences in outlook. By Story's standards, George was a radical. All radicals were dangerous. Therefore George was dangerous. That a radical should be in love with his younger daughter seemed to William Story even more dangerous. And if his daughter were in love with George . . . But it hadn't come to that yet. Or if it had, Emma was keeping it to herself.

In the fall of 1906, shortly after the reopening of the New York School of Art (whose classes George attended less diligently than he had during the two previous years), he followed Robert Henri's suggestion that he submit some examples of his work for possible display at the annual exhibition of the Pennsylvania Academy of Fine Arts in Philadelphia. Of the pieces he offered, two drawings were selected, the first of his work to be seen by the public outside of New York.

It was soon after this, in October or November, that George made the acquaintance, probably through Henri, of Hardesty Maratta, a chemist and paint manufacturer who was offering painters something entirely different in the way of materials—pre-mixed colors in tubes. Theretofore, a painter had had to blend each tone for himself from the three primary pigments and from black and white. Some artists were horrified by Maratta's innovation. Henri and Bellows were delighted, in spite of the fact that it necessitated a much larger palette, with individual receptacles for each shade.

With his new tray of assorted colors, of which he was very proud, Bellows painted his first nude figure (though he had made many drawings of the figure, male and female), a picture in dark tones that deployed light in a manner vaguely reminiscent of Rembrandt. He called it, simply, *Nude, Miss Bentham.* At approximately the same time, he made a drawing of a baseball scene whose title vividly evokes the subject matter: *Kill the Umpire.*

It was in the course of this autumn that Bellows received his first visit from William Merritt Chase—who may just have wanted to inquire why his pupil was attending so few classes at his school. What the older man made of the work George was doing we don't know with certainty. In all likelihood, he was lofty and condescending; the young artist had talent but, to judge from what he saw on display in the studio, there seemed little chance that Bellows would ever enjoy the kind of prestige among rich patrons that made life comfortable and pleasant for Chase.

But George Bellows seems not to have aspired to that sort of pleasant life, where one was compelled to cater to the whims of the wealthy in order to survive. He rejoiced in his feeling of independence and would have been very reluctant to sacrifice it in the name of "success"—for that sort of success, in Bellows' terms, would have been failure. The price he paid now for his refusal to learn to paint "pretty" pictures was a condition that was just one cut above penury. There were few occasions when he could afford to give himself and Emma an evening on the town. They managed to go with some frequency to the popular and inexpensive vaudeville shows. Much more rarely did they attend productions presented by "legitimate" theaters, and when they did, George sometimes embarrassed Emma by his loud criticisms of the plays they were watching; the quality of serious American drama in this first decade of this century was not very high.

For the first time since coming to New York, George was able (with some help from his father) to return to Columbus for Christmas. He was happy to be home; he had missed the comfortable, familiar surroundings—his ancient father, his corpulent mother, Laura and Ben Monett and their son Howard, the Joe Taylors, the easy, uncomplicated life of the relatively small midwestern city. For a little time, perhaps, he even regretted his decision two and a half years earlier to leave it. But he soon appreciated that nostalgia alone was no reason for him to change his mind and join his father in the construction business. There was, for one most important thing, too little to stimulate him there, intellectually or artistically. And it wasn't long before New York was calling him back.

Before leaving Columbus, George made two fine pictures. The first was a profoundly touching portrait of his father in his seventy-eighth year—bald, bearded, with deep, sad eyes that looked out on a world that his generation had certainly made and as certainly didn't understand any longer. His gnarled old hands rested on the handle of a cane.

The second picture was the more surprising work. George learned from friends that Socks Raymond, who had played baseball with him at Central High School and at Ohio State had suffered a complete nervous breakdown and was now confined to a mental hospital. These institutions were called "lunatic asylums" in 1906, and the patients were treated as if they were animals who had no clear idea of who they were, where they were, or why they were there. The care of mental patients in the early twentieth century was not a bit more enlightened than it had been two hundred years earlier, when the great Irish writer Jonathan Swift had been so appalled by the conditions he observed in London's Bethlehem Hospital, the "Bedlam" of which he was a governor, that he left his entire estate for the creation of St. Patrick's Hospital, in Dublin, where those suffering from mental and emotional disorders might receive more humane attention.

We may surmise from George's drawing, which he called *Dance in a Madhouse,* just what he saw during his visit to his old friend Socks Raymond. It clearly has its artistic inspiration in comparable pictures by the Spanish painter Goya, who drew and painted several versions of similar scenes. This little Bellows work is frightening and disturbing. Though he made a lithograph of it years later, he is not known to have depicted any other aspect of life in a mental hospital—for it obviously disturbed and frightened him, too.

George made the train journey back to New York with
mixed feelings, distressed by what he had seen in Columbus and by the frailty of his father, yet pleased by the
prospect of being with Emma and his artist friends once
again. It was in his character to plunge ahead, however,
without too many backward glances—and this is just what
he did. Following his custom of walking about the city, he
came upon the excavations that were getting under way for
the building of Pennsylvania Station, which extended over
two full city blocks. As Piranesi had done for the relics of
Imperial Rome, unearthed all over Italy during the eighteenth century, George Bellows now began to do for bur-
geoning New York. His first painting of the work being
done to construct Pennsylvania Station was accomplished
in January 1907. He would record the progress several times
in following years.

Other paintings that resulted from these wanderings were
of what are called "genre" scenes, images of "homely"
activities in the city—*Dogs, Early Morning* and a picture
to which he first gave the descriptive title *Niggers Having
a Tin Can Battle,* which he later altered to the wry *Battle
of San Juan Hill,* in reference to the Cuban charge led by
Teddy Roosevelt during the Spanish-American War. While
neither of these paintings is a masterpiece, both are strong
indications of George's continuing fascination with the street
life of New York.

His own existence, as he beheld it in the studio into
which he had moved only a few months earlier, was hectic
—in an amiable sort of way. The larger quarters were soon
filled with strays: friends, or friends of friends, who found
in its commodious warmth and atmosphere temporary and
even semi-permanent shelter from the cold of New York,
literal and figurative. Of those who established themselves
more or less firmly, the most unlikely seems to have been

Lloyd Grisby, who taught Latin at the Manlius School. Another was George Ferry, a gadabout Irish-American from Virginia who later dealt in high-priced real estate. And then there were innumerable visitors, most of them fellow painters, including Rockwell Kent, who was full of happy anecdotes of his summer on Monhegan Island in Maine.

Kent and Bellows were never to be the closest of friends —which may appear strange, since they shared not only a mutual concern for art but a common political philosophy (if, by 1907, Bellows can fairly be said to have formulated for himself so stable a thing as a "philosophy"). The difficulty may have been that Kent's was a far more forceful and dynamic personality than Bellows'. In any event, there was respect between them, and admiration of each other's work and ambitions, if not true intimacy. Bellows thought very highly of Kent's precise style, and if Kent thought George's work a bit amorphous in comparison with his own powerfully linear manner, he heartily approved of his subject matter as demonstration of a commitment to the problems of the "masses" and their unhappy lives.

It was fairly soon after his return from Columbus that George was invited by Ed Keefe to attend a prize fight in Tom Sharkey's saloon, just across Broadway from their studio in the Lincoln Arcade. Moses King, a New London acquaintance of Keefe's and currently lightweight champion of Connecticut, was to have a bout there. Prizefighting was illegal in New York in 1907, but like so many laws, it had its loopholes. In this case, the statute was circumvented by the simple device of converting Sharkey's into a club for the evening of the fight. The dues were nominal, but only members were permitted into the back room, where the bout was to be staged.

The immediate product of this initial exposure to the "manly art" was Bellows' first painting on the theme of boxing—the subject for which he is best known to posterity. Though he was to make many drawings and several lithographs of various prize-fight subjects, his reputation as the principal exponent of ring art is founded on only five paintings, in one of which, *Introducing John L. Sullivan,* made years after 1907, there is no boxing at all. These five canvases represent a very small fraction of Bellows' total output of seven or eight hundred paintings. Moreover, in the opinion of many, they are not his finest efforts.

In March, one of his paintings was selected by the jury of the National Academy of Design for its spring exhibition. Surprisingly, it was *River Rats,* chosen, we must suppose, for its charm rather than for its social commentary on the poverty of city children's lives. The art critic of *The Nation* gave it a favorable notice, the first praise the artist ever received from the press of the city in which he had decided to live and learn. In a showing of pictures by students of the Chase School in the following month, George exhibited three pictures that, though they attracted attention for their harsh observations of city life, were less happily treated by the press.

The March exhibition of the Academy had provoked the fury of Robert Henri. For though he, as a member, had been represented, paintings by the remaining seven artists who constituted "The Eight" had been excluded. Henri decided that he and his friends must stage an exhibition of their own. To this end, Henri made arrangements with William Macbeth, who operated a commercial gallery on Madison Avenue, to present a show of "The Eight" in February of the next year—the first month that the Macbeth Gallery was available.

Before this plan was made public, however, the press took note, in early May, of another event, which was of far greater significance in the eyes of the world—the trial of

William Dudley ("Big Bill") Haywood and two other men, all members of the Industrial Workers of the World, the "Wobblies," for conspiracy to murder the Governor of Idaho. Haywood, perfectly type-cast in the alternative roles of folk hero and folk villain, was defended by the most celebrated trial lawyer of the generation, Clarence Darrow, and eventually acquitted of all charges. But in the course of the hearings, many prominent Americans expressed their views about the justice or injustice of the accusations. It was hardly astonishing to find Haywood and his friends supported by Eugene Debs, leader of the Socialist party, and by the famous radical Russian novelist, Maxim Gorky. Nor was anyone startled by President Roosevelt's assertion, during the trial, that the accused were "guilty of incitement to, or apology for, bloodshed and violence." Though the Chief Executive said he was referring specifically to the bloody mining strike led by Haywood at Cripple Creek, Colorado, there was no doubt in anyone's mind that his words were intended to influence the jury in the conspiracy trial. Most puzzling, however, was Mark Twain's bitter condemnation of the defendants.

The trial was one of the most controversial in recent memory. Among reactions of powerful emotion produced in the larger cities throughout the country, it inspired two simultaneous parades in New York one evening in May, both in support of Haywood and his friends. Since the accused had been labeled "undesirable citizens," many of the marchers who proceeded along Lexington and Fifth avenues wore buttons that proclaimed, "I am an undesirable citizen." Among the paraders that night was George Bellows, not quite an "activist" as we understand that term today, but certainly a defender of activism. The American students of the sixties didn't invent protest, nor did they invent violence.

Neither his intermittent courtship of lovely Emma Story
nor his anxious concern over the fate of Big Bill Haywood
interrupted the flow of George Bellows' work. With the
coming of summer and the disappearance from the Broadway studio of Ed Keefe and Fred Cornell, he devoted some
of his time to the portrayal of the children of the neighborhood—*Jimmy Flanagan Laughing, Frankie the Organ Boy,*
and *The Little Girl in White,* the last a portrait of Queenie
Burnett, who picked up and delivered his laundry every
week. He also made a large drawing, *Knockout,* based on
his first night at Sharkey's the previous winter.

When the New York School of Art opened its doors
again in September, students returned to the city. Among
the new arrivals was a young man from Buffalo, Eugene
Speicher, who, like Bellows, was an enthusiastic athlete.
Indeed, the two first met not at the Chase School, but at
a YMCA gymnasium, where Speicher watched George playing basketball. When they had introduced themselves,
Speicher inquired if George was the Bellows who had
once played for the Ohio State varsity basketball team.
Art, it seems, never entered this conversation. Only a day
or two later, after they had become friendly, did they
meet again by chance in Chase's studio and realize that
they had a lot more in common than basketball. Eugene
Speicher became one of Bellows' closest friends and so
remained until George's death.

With an eye to humiliating the jury for the National
Academy of Design's next show, Robert Henri urged all
his friends and more proficient students to submit examples of their work. As he had fully expected (and even,
we may imagine, rather hoped), all the members of "The
Eight" save for himself saw their work rejected once again.
And once again, George Bellows was given a place on the
walls that academicians liked to consider hallowed. In

fact, the Academy this year accepted two of his recent paintings, *Pennsylvania Station Excavation* and *Club Night*, the picture based on his evening at Sharkey's. Both of these works were received with praise by a majority of the critics who mentioned them at all, although the observer for the *Journal* was unkind to *Club Night;* it was not, he suggested, suitable for framing.

Feeling that he might not see his father alive again if he delayed a trip to Columbus, George went home for Christmas in 1907. Soon after his arrival, he fell ill—a condition he reported gloomily to Emma, whose reply was hardly designed to improve his state of mind: "Your poor mother has my sincerest sympathy as I know exactly what you are like when you look like a funeral." He continued to look "like a funeral" for several weeks, to the delight of a mother who enjoyed having him at home and once again dependent on her ministrations. He recovered slowly, and when he was well enough to paint, he made another portrait of his old father, who was pleased with the finished work.

Just about the time of George's return to New York, in early February, the long awaited and much heralded exhibition of "The Eight" opened in the Macbeth Gallery on Madison Avenue. The reaction of the New York press was, on the whole, one of disappointment. Reviewers who had seen only the paintings of Henri in any quantity were rather let down by the pictures of the remaining seven. It was, they allowed, not nearly so outrageous as the conservative academicians had led them to believe. So the show was something less than a success of scandal and certainly not a financial triumph either. Only four thousand dollars worth of pictures were sold, though Robert Henri (nothing if not loyal to his friends) maintained that sales would have been appreciably higher had it not been for the recent stock-market crash. The only cry of pain had come from *Town Topics*, the most scurrilous social rag of the period, whose critic called the contributors to the exhibition "a revolutionary black gang," and added that they were "apostles of ugliness." From so disreputable but so widely read a source, comments like that were welcome—but they didn't help sales.

Nevertheless, this independent showing of the paintings of "The Eight" did make a point, at least insofar as the National Academy of Design was concerned. The jury of the Academy's spring show proved much more hospitable to their work when it was submitted for its spring show. In fact, "The Eight" was given a whole wall to itself, a development that was particularly gratifying to Henri, who had argued so long for a reasonable display of work by his seven associates. As we shall note, however, Henri's joy was to be of brief duration. For its next exhibition, the Academy reverted to type, and once again excluded all but Henri's work.

More pleasing to Bellows was the news that a painting he had only recently made, a view of the Hudson River from Riverside Drive, *North River*, accepted for this same exhibition at the Academy in the spring of 1908, had been given the Hallgarten second prize, the first such award the young artist had ever received, and no less welcome for the two hundred dollars that went along with it. The letter from the Academy's secretary, Harry Watrous, informing him of the jury's decision, concluded with a postscript in this important figure's own hand: "Keep up the good work, my boy. I have my eye on you."

We should pause here briefly and consider why it was that the Academy should have thought so highly of Bellows' work, which it had accepted for exhibition from his second year in New York, when it cherished so poor a view of the paintings of Glackens, Sloan, Shinn, Luks, Lawson, Prendergast, and Davies—men ten years more experienced (and presumably, therefore, more skilled) than George. One is immediately inclined to look for possible sources of influence that Bellows might have had with the Academy's juries; but the search is fruitless. He had only one friend at this court, Robert Henri, who was the eighth member of the excluded "Eight." A glance at the paintings the Academy accepted from George's brush for display is not much more helpful. He was no less an "apostle of ugliness" than the banned artists. If George had secret help among members of the Academy, the secret has been kept to this day; his familiarity with Watrous was casual at best, and we have seen how effective Henri's friendship could be, as far as Academy policy was concerned. It is a puzzle that remains unsolved.

George, in any case, didn't need the eye of Harry Watrous to induce him to continue painting in his own way. During the spring months of 1908 he made a number of small oils, including *Up the River* and *Steaming Streets* —the latter of a winter scene absolutely unique to New York, beneath whose asphalt pavements run the pipes of the City Steam Company, a private utility supplying heat to a number of buildings in the midtown Manhattan area. In winter, the streets of this section of town still steam.

With the closing of the New York School of Art in June, Robert Henri departed for Spain, as had become his custom, bringing along with him a group of handsome young ladies—art students intent (more or less) on improving themselves culturally and even, perhaps, matrimonially, for all were well aware of their good-looking teacher's marital eligibility. Their consternation could scarcely have been greater than that of Henri's friends when they learned, several weeks later, that before leaving New York, he had married one of the girls, the beautiful Marjorie Organ.

Though the subject of marriage was still very much on Bellows' mind that summer, his prospects remained dim. He was far from being in a position to support even himself, let alone a wife. The topic was not often discussed, because there was nothing much to be said. During the last weeks of June and the first ones of July, he and Emma took as much pleasure as they could find in walks through Central Park, visits to the Metropolitan Museum of Art, and, by way of comic relief, to Coney Island. Both were disconsolate at times, for this was the only part of the holidays they could share. George had accepted an offer to teach a course in painting at the University of Virginia, and Emma was to join her family once again in Nova Scotia.

Though he mightily regretted having to leave her, the possibility of earning some money by his journey to Charlottesville, arranged (it is thought) by his friend from that town, George Ferry, was too tempting to reject. But by the time he had paid his fare down and back and taken care of his personal expenses while in residence there, George netted not a penny more than five dollars from the venture, and during his stay accomplished only a single painting, *Virginia Horse Show*, which remained unsold at the time of his death. He did make some sketches out of which grew another picture that sold during his lifetime, but taken all in all, his weeks in the South were among the most miserable of his life. Not even a fortnight with his distant relatives at Sag Harbor, where the air was trim and fresh and the sea cool, could brighten his outlook very much—for he missed Emma. Nor did she make life more bearable for him with her habitually tormenting references to the attentions lavished on her by the young doctor whom she once more had encountered in Nova Scotia. It seemed a summer that would never end.

But it did end, and when he resumed his work in New York that fall, it was to make a number of paintings of a rare new quality, quite different in style from his earlier pictures, bolder and stronger. In a brusque, almost harsh manner that owed its inspiration to Henri (but which George had adapted to his own special vigor), he painted two fine portraits, one of Jimmy Flanagan (*Red-faced Boy Laughing*) and another of Jimmy's cousin Paddy (*Boy with Bare Chest*), both strikingly reminiscent in their spontaneous joy of the snapshot-like portraits of Frans Hals, the Dutch master of the seventeenth century.

Later, in the early winter months, George returned to the site of the Pennsylvania Station excavations, this time after dark, and made, as a result of several excursions there, *Excavation at Night*. "That picture," he later observed, "is the best attempt I ever made to locate the center of interest by strong light. . . ." And once more as well, the artist turned to the mighty Hudson for inspiration, producing *Rain on the River*.

About a month before Christmas, a friend of George's from Cleveland made arrangements to exhibit *Club Night*, the painting of the prize fight in Sharkey's saloon, in that city's Athletic Club, a location that would seem ideal for it. However, after only a few days of exposure, it was removed at the order of the club's directors, who explained with some embarrassment to Bellows that the scene was causing distress to the lady guests. On his way to Columbus for the holidays, the artist, caught between the opposed emotions of rage and amusement, took possession of the painting and brought it with him to his home. We have no record of the impression the picture made on the Bellows family at this time, but it was not displayed in the city on this occasion. While in Columbus, George explored with his old friend Joe Taylor the possibility of obtaining some portrait commissions through the university or its alumni association. Though the professor could promise nothing, he naturally agreed to do what he could—but it was some time before his efforts produced results.

A number of developments greeted Bellows on his return to New York in January 1909. The most startling news was that William Merritt Chase's New York School of Art had closed its doors forever, a victim of the ailment that besets almost every private institution, a chronic shortage of funds. Most of the instructors had failed to receive their salaries for the fall term, and they were by no means Chase's only creditors. Among those suddenly without teaching employment was, of course, Robert Henri. He promptly opened a school of his own in a studio on the same floor as that occupied by Bellows and his friends at 1947 Broadway.

Among the new tenants of the Bellows studio this year was Eugene O'Neill, a friend of Ed Keefe's from New London, son of the well-known actor and alcoholic James O'Neill, who would pass his love of the stage and of whiskey on to his famous progeny. If the young O'Neill had at this time any interest in the theater, however, he was concealing it well from his acquaintances. Having been banished from the family home in Connecticut by a father who thought him worthless at best, he was scratching a sporadic living from the door-to-door sale of cheap costume jewelry. From this experience, we may imagine, he was able to draw useful material for the creation of the central character of *The Iceman Cometh*. But such intimations were unknown in the winter of 1909.

Emma Story was terrified of Eugene O'Neill. He had a reputation as a conscientious womanizer that he made no effort to conceal. She always refused to visit the studio in the Lincoln Arcade if O'Neill was there by himself. And when, at the end of January, George and Ed Keefe joined Eugene at his father's summer house at Zion, New Jersey, for an uncomfortable and (so far as Bellows was concerned) unsatisfactory winter vacation, she addressed her letters to "Decadence Manor." Precisely what George thought he would be able to achieve near the New Jersey shore at this season of the year is difficult to imagine, but the experience was in all ways a disappointment. He was back in New York and painting once again by the middle of February.

In March he made a return visit to the construction site of Pennsylvania Station. Two paintings resulted from this visit, the most notable being *Blue Morning.* But more important for Bellows' pride and purse, it was in this month, too, that he actually sold a picture, *North River,* to the Pennsylvania Academy of Fine Arts, for the immense sum of two hundred and fifty dollars. There was another surprise in store. After the spring exhibition of the National Academy of Design in New York (in which his work had been shown but given no awards), George was astounded to receive a letter from Harry Watrous, secretary of the Academy, announcing Bellows' election as an associate of that illustrious body. Watrous' eye had indeed been on him, as he had promised the year before. But why? No answer emerges. In spite of the fact that he despised the Academy for its neglect of "The Eight" and other contemporaries, he followed Robert Henri's example and accepted the offer of membership. Like Henri, he hoped that by affiliating himself with the hidebound conservatives, he could change their views; he thought it better to bore from within than to wail from without. Besides, from a purely financial standpoint, associate membership would enhance his reputation and make his paintings more salable. And financial considerations were of great moment to a young man of twenty-seven who wanted to get married and who, in the spring of 1909, had sold exactly one picture.

His election as an associate of the Academy did have one curious outcome—an invitation to visit the studio home of Cecilia Beaux. Miss Beaux, a full academician with Paris training and a very fashionable reputation as a portrait painter (second only in magnitude among American artists to John Singer Sargent, who worked mostly in London), bestowed her invitations with some frugality. So once more we are confronted by a puzzling question: Why did she express an interest in George Bellows? The atmosphere with which this Philadelphia maiden in her middle forties surrounded herself could not have been more different from any other the young man had discovered in New York. Was it, then, his manly appearance, his prowess as an athlete, his kindliness? It certainly couldn't have been that she was a great admirer of his work, for the painting of Cecilia Beaux could scarcely be more removed from George's; hers was a polite, easily digested style that never got in anyone's way—nor ever stuck in anyone's mind.

In Miss Beaux's salon George found no rebellion, artistic or political. He must have felt out of place at once, though he was no boor and undoubtedly conducted himself like the gentleman he was. But neither was he a sycophant. Had he ever chosen to follow the easy path to popular and financial success, Cecilia Beaux could certainly have facilitated his progress in that direction. This must surely have been in her mind. But such was not George's inclination. A social being he definitely was, but not a "society" being. And this would prove just as well, for when he was well enough known to receive requests from the prosperous for portraits, he frequently failed to produce what was required. "Society" wasn't his style at all.

He wasn't a creature of what the socialists and anarchists among his friends were calling the "proletariat," those disinherited or dispossessed by the social order of the day, but no more was he a man to be easily seduced by the idea of his era's equivalent of "the beautiful people." He was and would remain, quite simply, his own man, destined to follow his own star. He was mildly diverted and even a little flattered to be asked occasionally to take tea with Cecilia Beaux, and until the summer, he did it with some frequency. But it was inevitable that he and she should sooner or later lose interest in each other.

In April, Joe Taylor wrote from Columbus that he had secured a commission for George to paint for Ohio State University the portrait of Professor James Canfield, who came East for the purpose and posed several times in the uproarious, squalid studio on Broadway. What the retiring scholar made of the artist and his workshop we can only conjecture, but when the finished painting was shipped back to Columbus, Taylor reacted to it with extravagant pleasure: "So great things are painted. It is lighted in Rembrandt's daring manner, achieved with something of Velasquez's just balance of color." After such a song of praise, it is regrettable to have to state that it is a very respectable likeness of the professor—and not much more than that. Portraits to order were not George Bellows' forte.

Though there were other exhibitions to which he contributed in the course of this spring, the implications of one in particular seemed pretty dazzling to a young man from Ohio who had never ventured outside the United States and who never would. George was among fifty American artists invited to send work to a show that was to be hung in Venice. The Italian correspondent of the

Boston *Transcript* commented favorably on his contribution, giving it as his opinion that George Bellows showed promise.

It was, however, beginning to be clear that he would not be able much longer to survive on occasional awards and even-less-frequent sales. He must, if he were ever to convince Emma (and perhaps even more difficult, Emma's father) that he would make a suitable husband, make some marked financial progress. Otherwise, he would have to seek more-gainful employment. Fortunately, there were happy omens. At the spring exhibition of the Carnegie Institute in Pittsburgh, whose jury had rejected one of the two pictures George had submitted, the second offering, *Forty-two Kids,* was sold for three hundred dollars. It was hardly enough to get married on, but at least he wouldn't starve over the summer, which was near at hand.

He remained for most of July and August in New York, deserted by Eugene O'Neill and, much to his sorrow, by Ed Keefe, who had at last decided to renounce all further efforts to become a professional painter in favor of the security of a career in architecture in his father's firm. George missed him especially that summer, because he knew he wasn't coming back in the fall. In July, he made a brief visit to Sag Harbor, where his parents were vacationing, and found his father frailer—but this process was continuous, and hardly amazing in a man over eighty.

Back in the city, George painted two totally different pictures simultaneously—*Summer Night,* another of his urban "mood" pieces, and *Stage at Sharkey's,* a second and more ambitious oil of prize fighting in the back room of the saloon across the street. As its title suggests, these evening entertainments were for men only—a fact that may seem less surprising if we recall that until the advent of Prohibition in 1919, women rarely entered public bars except to extract their husbands. And prize fighting was still against the law except, as at Sharkey's, if it was conducted under the auspices of a fictitious club.

George and Emma saw a little of each other that summer; he accompanied her, with a chaperone, to Point Pleasant, New Jersey, for a weekend. But as the autumn arrived, there was still nothing more definite about their relationship (after nearly four years) than a mutual but mute understanding that one day they might marry.

In September, the share of the rent for the studio that had been Ed Keefe's was now paid by Ted Ireland, an art student from Columbus who later became a close friend of Eugene O'Neill. O'Neill himself drifted into the studio for visits whenever he was in town. Another newcomer to the group that congregated here was Ben Ali Haggin, a New Yorker who was studying down the hall with Robert Henri. Haggin's home became a haven for George and Emma and all the artists to whom the young man was attracted. His mother was a wonderful cook and an accomplished musician. In a day when neither radio nor television was available for entertainment, there was only music for diversion, the homemade variety or that provided by phonograph records that were, to our ears accustomed to high-fidelity reproduction, indescribably harsh and shrill —of very low fidelity.

The first encouragement that Emma offered George's long-blighted courtship occurred at about this time, when she wrote to ask him to take her to see the fortieth anniversary exhibition of the Metropolitan Museum of Art. "I want to see the pictures very much and would rather go with you than any one else . . . you are very, very sweet and I give just one rap about you." One rap, in Emma's own handwriting, was far better than no rap at all. But it

hardly constituted a wholehearted endorsement of his proposal of marriage.

Another evening at Sharkey's that autumn produced the
third of George's paintings on the boxing theme. This one,
which many authorities on his work consider his best in this
genre, was originally called *A Nigger and a White Man,* an
unfortunate but accurate description of the scene. Its final
title, *Both Members of This Club,* was almost certainly intended as an ironic commentary on the issue of race (despite the original title), and also on the practice of making
the boxers temporary members of Sharkey's club in order
that the fight could take place within the bounds of the
absurd law.

Three other paintings of this season reflect different aspects of Bellows' widening range of subject matter. *The
Bridge, Blackwell's Island* depicts the last stages of construction of the Queensborough Bridge, which connects
Manhattan with Long Island City—a variation on the
Pennsylvania Station theme he had so often treated. *Lone
Tenement,* as the title suggests, is a sad little picture whose
message is just as intelligible to us today as it was in the
autumn of 1909—a single, decrepit building, standing in
an open space that has been cleared for new construction.
Were it not for the soft, almost misty technique Bellows
employed, the picture could have been created yesterday;
it conveys one of the many doleful sides of urban slum
life, the devastation and emptiness. The third painting, one
that he had begun in the summer of 1908 when he and
Emma had gone to Coney Island, was *Beach at Coney
Island.* It foreshadows a number of paintings, by Glackens
and by younger artists influenced by Bellows, that depicted
the crowds seeking refuge from the suffocating city on
the sands of Jamaica Bay.

The closest he came to making a sale of his work before

the Christmas holiday was an offer to contribute some drawings to *The Craftsman,* a magazine of the arts. Bellows' sketches appeared in the publication, along with those of Glackens, Sloan, and Shinn. Robert Henri organized an exhibition for "The Eight" and their artistic allies at the MacDowell Club in December. Two of George's paintings were displayed, *Laughing Boy* and *Rain on the River;* they received praise but were not sold.

Though he was unable as yet to see the fruit that would finally ripen, George Bellows had been a part of the art world of New York long enough to appreciate that the tree from which all fruit sprang was called "exposure." It almost didn't matter where one's work was seen so long as it was reasonably well displayed and the artist's name was spelled correctly. While he was home for Christmas that year, George thought the time right for him to arrange an exhibition of his own work and that of his master, Robert Henri.

Backed by the faithful Joe Taylor, he approached the directors of the Carnegie Library in Columbus. They eagerly assented to the proposal. But when Bellows insisted, because the natural light available in the exhibition rooms was inadequate, that newfangled incandescent lamps should be installed, the board flatly refused. They balked initially at the expense of the project, and were not impressed when George pointed out that, once in place, the new lighting could be used again and again. He suspected that a more basic reason for their reluctance was simple conservatism. Artificial light had yet to be used, for example, in any public gallery in New York. Columbus' timid art enthusiasts were not about to be the first in the Middle West to take so bold and therefore so controversial a step. On this unhappy note, George headed back to New York. He even had an additional tribulation to mull over in his mind—his growing baldness, about which his mother, who had seen him as recently as the previous July, had expressed horror on his arrival in Columbus for the holidays.

Within ten days or so of his return to the city, George forgot the foot-dragging of the board members of the Carnegie Library in Columbus, and even forgot that he was rapidly losing most of his hair—for he had so many more-important things to consider and because vanity was not one of his faults. The Pennsylvania Academy of Fine Arts accepted five of his paintings for its next exhibition, more pictures than he had ever shown before in such a gallery. The selection of work that he sent, reflecting his whole gamut of subject matter, was very well received in Philadelphia—though not without reservations.

Yet the fact remained that he was now being accorded far more massive exposure than every member of "The Eight" except for Henri. A further indication of his growing reputation came from Hugo Reisinger, a rich German-American who had, the previous year, organized an exhibition in New York of contemporary German art, and now proposed to reverse the procedure by transporting a comparable show of American work to Berlin, in the hope of effecting a closer cultural understanding between the artists and intellectuals of the two countries. George Bellows' paintings were to be included. The painter submitted two of his most recent canvases, *Summer Night* and *The Bridge, Blackwell's Island*. Though there could be no way for him to know it, this connection with Reisinger would, within the month, prove even more important to him.

The National Arts Club, anxious that its reputation not be identical to that of the National Academy of Design because of a refusal to show hospitality to the work of younger artists, undertook in February 1910 an exhibition devoted entirely to products of the new generation. In addition to all the members of "The Eight," the club displayed paintings by John Marin, Marsden Hartley, and Alfred Henry Maurer, all of whom were of middle age—and therefore "new," as distinguished from the old fossils of the Academy. George was one of the very youngest artists represented, and for this exhibition, which he judged very important because it was a sharp departure from National Arts Club practice and because it was occurring in New York, where the chief market for paintings was, he chose pictures that he believed would not antagonize potential patrons—*Winter Afternoon,* one of his finer New York scenes, which drew critical applause, and *Morning Snow,* immediately purchased by Hugo Reisinger for five hundred dollars, the highest price yet paid for a Bellows. It was a great moment when he learned of Reisinger's decision.

When the jury for the National Academy of Design exhibition had made its selection for the spring show, it was clear that the good intentions manifested the previous year, and the prodding of the display at the National Arts Club, were to be ignored. With a zeal that was becoming intolerable, the committee rejected the submissions of all members of "The Eight" except for Henri, whose work, like Bellows', could not be excluded, because both were members of the Academy. The conservatives had been shocked, quite genuinely, by the work hung in the Academy's halls in the spring of 1909. They knew very well what art was; art was beauty, and what Henri's friends were painting was ugliness. Just why George Bellows, who was no less an advocate of the new look in painting than most of "The Eight," should have been exempted from such criticism is a mystery. Like most clubs, the Academy kept no written records of its debates on such subjects.

When the selection to be shown by the Academy was made known, Robert Henri was enraged—once again; and once again he proposed to do something about it. He planned to put on an exhibition of his own, beginning April 1, in a rented brownstone house in West Thirty-fourth Street. The show would be open to all artists. Moreover, any work submitted would be displayed, subject only to a fee of ten dollars per item. The arrangement would be alphabetical. It was a co-operative venture that enlisted the enthusiastic support of many younger painters and sculptors, who helped with the complete refurbishing of the house, an operation that included the installation of artificial lighting—the first in New York. Of the six hundred pictures and sculptures shown, one alone was displayed out of its alphabetical order, Robert Henri's graceful portrait of his beautiful young wife Marjorie, which was (as was altogether proper) accorded the place of honor facing the entrance.

Miraculously (given the brief time allowed for the extensive preparations), the opening of the first Independent Show, as it was called, took place on the appointed day. The press, which had been kept informed by almost daily reports from those who were taking part in it and those who were loudly opposing it, was astounded not only by the extraordinary number and variety of works exhibited, but by the dimensions of the crowd lined up on Thirty-fourth Street for an opportunity to view them. Something approaching two thousand people paid a modest admission charge on the first day to see this exhibition that the papers had so widely publicized.

Critics were vociferous—and confused. With so many different kinds of art to take into account, they were unable to find a single generalization that would cover them all. Inevitably, many fell back on the cliché, "Things will never be the same again." But it wasn't very clear what the writers were referring to—for some wrote more about the

1) DANCE IN A MADHOUSE, 1906. Courtesy of The Art Institute of Chicago, Charles H. and Mary F. S. Worcester Collection.

2) PORTRAIT OF MY FATHER, 1906. The Columbus Gallery of Fine Arts, Columbus, Ohio: Gift of Howard B. Monnett.

3) TIN CAN BATTLE, SAN JUAN HILL, NEW YORK, 1907. F. M. Hall Collection, University of Nebraska, Lincoln.

4) POLO, 1907. From the Collection of Mr. and Mrs. John Hay Whitney.

5) CLUB NIGHT, 1907. From the Collection of Mr. and Mrs. John Hay Whitney.

6) FORTY-TWO KIDS, 1907. In the collection of The Corcoran Gallery of Art.

7) THE LONE TENEMENT, 1909. National Gallery of Art, Washington, D. C., Gift of Chester Dale.

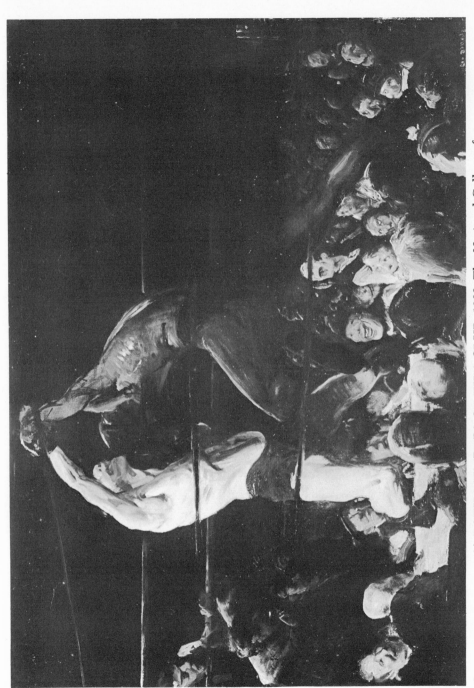

8) BOTH MEMBERS OF THIS CLUB, 1909. The National Gallery of Art, Washington, D. C., Gift of Chester Dale.

9) THE BRIDGE, BLACKWELL'S ISLAND, 1909. The Toledo Museum of Art, Toledo, Ohio, Gift of Edward Drummond Libbey, 1912.

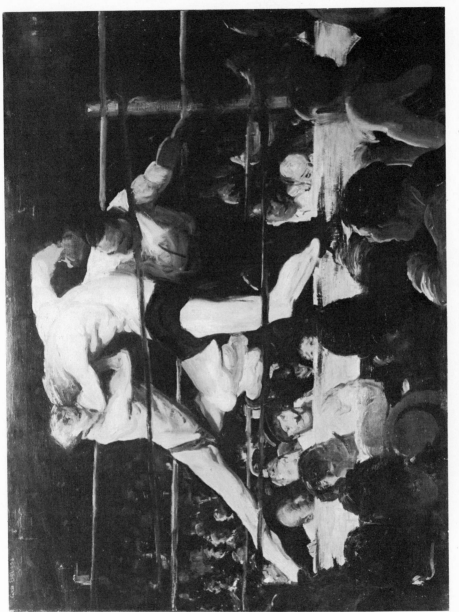

10) STAG AT SHARKEY'S, 1909. The Cleveland Museum of Art, Purchased for the Hinman B. Hurlbut Collection.

11) POLO AT LAKEWOOD, 1910. The Columbus Gallery of Fine Arts, Columbus, Ohio.

12) MEN OF THE DOCKS, 1912. Springfield Museum of Fine Arts, Springfield, Massachusetts.

13) OUTSIDE THE BIG TENT, 1912. Addison Gallery of American Art, Phillips Academy, Andover, Massachusetts.

14) THE CIRCUS, 1912. Addison Gallery of American Art, Phillips Academy, Andover, Massachusetts.

6　Sunlit Surf
Oct 1913
oil 15 x 19½
P R RO Y B
Price 400
Lux Monterey 1914
Chicago Art Inst 1914
Los Angeles 1915
San Francisco 1915
Detroit 1915
Cincinnati 1915
Minneapolis 1915
Hackley 1915
Wooster 1915
Perkins Chicago
O Brien
Thurber Gal

15) Copy of a page from Bellows' notebook, 1913. Courtesy H. V. Allison & Company, Inc.

16) CLIFF DWELLERS, 1913. Los Angeles County Museum of Art, Los Angeles County Funds.

17) THE SAWDUST TRAIL, 1916. Layton Art Gallery Collection, Milwaukee Art Center.

18) **THE DRUNK**, 1917. Addison Gallery of American Art, Phillips Academy, Andover, Massachusetts.

rowdy spectators (an unusual and gratifying occurrence in itself, for New York art shows were still considered the domain of the rich) than about the paintings and sculptures to be seen.

For all its great notoriety, the Independent Show was not a financial success. Very few paintings were sold. George Bellows, who had submitted eight pieces in all, sold three drawings for a total of five hundred dollars to Joseph B. Thomas, the second private collector to express a serious interest in his art. Thus, within the space of only two months, the artist realized one thousand dollars from sales, almost twice as much as he had earned in this way during the entire five years and more of his career until March of 1910. Nor was this the last happy event of the season; three more were to come. The first was his nomination to life membership in the National Arts Club, an honor without immediate monetary value but one that could only help his prestige. The second, of which he learned on May 14, was his designation as instructor at the Art Students League of New York for the next academic year, a post he had applied for without much hope of success. The salary was one thousand dollars.

The third and most momentous occurrence of that spring was, to a degree, an outgrowth of all the pleasant things that had happened to him before. Emma agreed in principle to become his wife in the relatively near future—and although the wedding date was far from definite, George felt that this new and stunning change in all his affairs amply justified his asking his father for a "loan" with which to buy a house in New York. The elder George Bellows was probably not much more convinced in 1910 than he had been in 1904 that a life in art was anything like so promising financially as one in architecture, but he could only have respect for his son's indomitable persistence in the pursuit of his chosen profession, and must have been pleased and proud about the increasing tokens of recognition and success that were being accorded him. Apparently, he advanced George the sum of ten thousand dollars at once. Technically speaking, it was a loan, but the father of eighty-three and the son of twenty-eight were equally aware that at law such debts were unenforceable; the loan was in fact a gift. George never repaid it; his father never asked to be repaid.

Since Emma was to share his future life, George thought it only right that she should help him make the choice of the house in which they would live together—after he had reduced the range of possible locations to two, both in East Nineteenth Street, a block south of Gramercy Park. Without hesitation, Emma selected the house at 146 East Nineteenth Street, a sturdy brick structure built about seventy-five years before. It could easily be renovated to provide an apartment whose rental would help defray the costs of maintenance and taxes, and a studio for George on the top floor.

Until the tenants of the house he had just purchased departed in June, George occupied the better part of his time in making plans for the changes he meant to effect. He would do most of the work himself because, as he pointed out with pride to Emma, he was qualified by many summers' experience to do all sorts of construction work. And when she responded, as she surely must have, that he would probably find it more economical to pay professionals to do the job while he devoted himself to art, he doubtless replied that he needed to do as much of the work as possible, needed to because it was to be *their* house. There was, he acknowledged, one major bit of reconstruction that he would have to leave to others, the raising of the roof by eight feet to make room in the attic for a two-story studio.

After five years of dealing with George Bellows, Emma Story knew her man well enough to give in, and even perhaps to rejoice in his desire to have a major hand in the creation of the nest they soon would share.

In the meantime, the artist did allow himself to be lured for a few days to the Lakewood, New Jersey, home of his new patron, Joseph Thomas. There, for the first time, he had an opportunity to observe for some hours one of the favorite pastimes of the horsy rich, polo; he made many sketches of the furious action of this exclusive and expensive sport. On his return to New York, he painted two pictures based on his little studies—*Polo at Lakewood*, which Robert Henri immediately pronounced the finest picture he had yet created, and *Spring Idlers*, of which his friend and former master held a high but somewhat inferior opinion. He made only one other painting that spring, *Warships on the Hudson*, in which he recorded a Memorial Day visit of a part of the U.S. fleet that had participated in the Spanish-American War and later toured the world. The picture is not at all warlike or even remotely military; it is a characteristic Bellows river scene.

From late June until the end of September, the artist was occupied with the renovations to his house in Nineteenth Street. Although Emma had still not set the date for their wedding, she gave him a little more encouragement in August when she wrote: "I have just awakened and my thoughts are in a state of chaos more or less. I haven't two consecutive ideas about any thing [sic] except you. . . ." It was only toward the middle of September that Emma hinted to a close friend that she and George might get married on the twenty-third of that month.

Marriage: First Years

The arrangements for the wedding ceremony were just as casual as Emma's report that it might take place on September 23. George, who had by this time wholly abandoned Methodism or any other sort of organized religion, would have preferred to be married by a justice of the peace. The Christian Scientists (whose leader, Mary Baker Eddy, had died that year) acknowledged no ministers and consequently had no wedding ceremony as such. But Emma thought a civil ceremony much too lacking in spirituality. Ultimately, she and George agreed on a church wedding to be performed by their friend Arthur Ketchum, a rather unorthodox Episcopal clergyman whose parish was in the South Bronx.

There were other complications. Although George's parents were just ending their holidays at Sag Harbor, he felt they should not be invited—not because he didn't want them present, but because he believed the journey would be too much of a strain for his aged father. The Storys, however, were invited and put in an appearance, despite William Story's misgivings about having a painter for a son-in-law.

The question that was uppermost in everyone's mind on the morning of September 23, 1910, was whether or not the bridegroom would get to the church on time. When

Emma flouted the tradition that prohibits the bride from seeing the prospective husband on the day of the ceremony and went to 146 East Nineteenth Street to see if George was ready, she found him hard at work on the alterations to the house. It was with some difficulty that she convinced him that he must bathe and change. Finally, with a handful of mutual friends, they made the long journey to the Bronx by subway and trolley car. The service was duly performed, but at an hour so late in the afternoon that the couple had to take a taxi back down to Manhattan in order to catch the last train for eastern Long Island, an expense for which George had not allowed.

They spent their wedding night at Montauk, at the easternmost point of Long Island, and the next day traveled the twenty-odd miles westward to Sag Harbor, where George presented Emma to his parents and to Laura and Ben Monett. The couple accepted the congratulations of the elder Bellowses. Afterward, with much embarrassment, the artist borrowed from his father enough money to pay for the trip back to New York, which he and Emma made the next morning. It was an appropriately chaotic beginning for a hectic and rather marvelous marriage.

One of the reasons why there are so many jokes and clichés about marriage is that the relationship lends itself readily to this kind of comment. The wonder is not that there are so many divorces and separations, but rather that so many marriages survive. And this seems trebly true of marriages between people who, because of the customs and inhibitions of their time and upbringing, hardly know each other before their wedding day. An illustration of the good sense and good fortune that Emma and George brought to *their* marriage is that though they quarreled about many things whose importance was only occasionally major, they preserved an atmosphere of good humor and remained an absolutely devoted and faithful couple in a Bohemian society that didn't hold a very high regard for either devotion or marital fidelity. For all that, within this new framework of matrimony that they had at last chosen for themselves after so many years of Emma's hesitations, they remained, as well, invincibly themselves; neither made any great effort to change the nature or habits of the other.

They continued their honeymoon at 146 East Nineteenth Street, where Emma Bellows (as she reluctantly agreed to call herself, despite her agreement in principle with the feminist Lucy Stone, who argued that for a woman to renounce her maiden name was an act of personal renunciation as well) adapted herself with commendable ease to married life. They entertained their friends—the Henris, the Glackenses, the Sloans, the Speichers. Soon after their marriage, George met the painter Leon Kroll, with whom he disagreed vigorously about almost everything having to do with art, particularly the use of color, but who nevertheless became a close friend.

The Bellows house was like the people who occupied it—open, friendly, warm, full of easy life and high humor. It attracted a strangely mixed group, apart from the artists whom one would normally expect to find there. The very rich Gertrude Vanderbilt Whitney quite probably made the acquaintance there of Miss Emma Goldman, the fierce, Russian-born anarchist who, along with her sometime lover Alexander Berkman, had been editing a radical periodical, *Mother Earth*, for the past four years. Mrs. Whitney was an important patron of the arts. Miss Goldman's interest in art was negligible, but as one of the founders of the Ferrer School in New York (named for a Spanish anarchist executed in 1909 for alleged complicity in a civil uprising in Barcelona), she had persuaded Bellows and John Sloan to give up a few hours each week to the teaching of art to underprivileged children who attended this institution. For in spite of his increasing acceptance by the people who could afford to purchase his paintings, George was still a radical in his politics and would keep his close sympathy for the anarchist movement until the entry of the United States into World War I.

When the Bellowses weren't entertaining of an evening or being entertained by others, they attended concerts, the theater, and the opera. One of their favorite resorts was still the home of young Ben Ali Haggin, where music was almost as intense a common bond as art. George was so fond of Haggin's mother that he presented her with the first painting that he made after his marriage, *Montauk Light and Point,* his initial experiment with a kind of work that he would happily continue for the rest of his life—landscapes and seascapes. In gratitude for this gift and out of her great affection for the couple, Mrs. Haggin offered George and Emma the use of her Catskill mountain retreat at Onteora. There they passed a tranquil week before the opening of the Art Students League.

While George was involved with his teaching and his painting, he managed to find time as well to begin a journal/catalog of his work, annotating each item with the date of its completion, the dimensions, the medium in which it was done, the exhibitions in which it was shown, and the price it brought if sold during his lifetime. This volume has proved an invaluable aid to Bellows scholars, who have, as a result of having it for consultation, been able to date every significant Bellows work.

Of the paintings he accomplished during the final months of 1910, three merit attention—*Blue Snow, the Battery* (which an early critic irreverently retitled "Assault and

Battery"—although it is difficult, seeing it now through eyes accustomed to far more violent painting, to comprehend this reaction); *Shore House,* a recollection of Montauk that is a kind of country cousin to *Lone Tenement* in its treatment of space and architecture; and finally, a third picture based on his short visit to Lakewood the previous summer, *Crowd at Polo.* To the exhibition of American painting in Berlin that was arranged by Hugo Reisinger, the British critic C. Lewis Hind responded by singling out Bellows' work for favorable comment, comparing it with the best of Winslow Homer—an analogy for which George was grateful, for he much admired Homer's painting.

George's anarchist friend Emma Goldman, in private and in print, was on the record as opposed to all forms of censorship—a position that was to receive more or less general acceptance in this country only a half century later—and Bellows supported her, though he confessed that he would, himself, feel quite uncomfortable walking down Fifth Avenue stark naked, as Miss Goldman asserted was every individual's perfect right; nonetheless, she conceded that such a whim seemed to her absurd. But freedom to behave seriously implied the similar freedom to be ridiculous.

Bellows, however, had more immediate concerns as the year 1911 began. He and Emma attended the opening of his first one-man show, at the Madison Gallery. It was a critical success, on the whole, and showed the young painter to be firmly established as a leader of a school of art to which, as yet, no name had been given. This exhibition offered a collection of two dozen paintings accomplished over the previous five years; critics and patrons of the arts were able to discover in them a growing skill and self-confidence, the presence of the whole personality of a man preoccupied at once with the craft of painting as such and with the capacity of art to convey a particular political and social point of view. The impact of George Bellows' art, as demonstrated in this show, was forceful and individual. If the earliest works on display disclosed a substantial debt to the manner of Robert Henri, the later paintings revealed his breaking away—establishing his own style, his own identity.

Coincidental with the opening of the exhibition at the Madison Gallery there came a bit of news that George and Emma received with quite different emotions. She was pregnant. George was delighted. Emma was annoyed; she was even, at first, furious. She had well understood her husband's desire to have children, but her apprehensions about pregnancy and childbirth (inspired in large measure by her Christian Science upbringing, which denied the value of medical assistance) were so great that she proposed the adoption of children rather than the manufacture of their own, a suggestion that George rejected hotly. She informed him that the baby would arrive in the early fall.

The success of the New York show influenced the directors of the Carnegie Library in Columbus to reconsider their refusal of the previous year to install artificial lighting. In exchange for this concession, George promised to organize for his home city an exhibition not only of his own work but of all the members of "The Eight" as well. In February, he and Emma went to Columbus, where he supervised the hanging of the first showing of contemporary art to be seen in the Ohio capital.

From his arrival, however, he encountered resistance from the directors of the library, who were "appalled" by the "frankness" of some of the paintings that Bellows had shipped out to them. In particular were they offended by his large drawing *Knockout*, by four nudes from the brush of Arthur B. Davies, and by a group of John Sloan's etchings, all of which they originally rejected altogether. When George threatened to cancel the entire show, the timid men of Columbus agreed to a compromise: all the works to which they objected were placed in a room whose door was bolted and guarded, accessible only to adult males— "the chamber of obscenities," as it was immediately dubbed by everyone who knew of it, which was almost every visitor.

To mark the opening of the exhibition, Robert Henri delivered an address. Like too many teachers, he was capable of speaking almost indefinitely if not interrupted, and in this instance he droned on for two hours. Despite the torpor that thus marked the unveiling of this show that seemed a spectacular novelty in the Ohio city, it was a popular success. As if to compensate George for the offense of hiding *Knockout* from the eyes of the "innocent," the Columbus Art Association purchased *Polo at Lakewood* for nine hundred dollars, almost double the price he had received for his most expensive painting barely a year earlier. The local boy had made good in his home town.

In his balconied studio in New York once more, with the arrival of the spring, Bellows returned to work with renewed energy and painted a variety of pictures on themes he had made familiar—*The Docks in Winter, Mardi Gras at Coney Island, Snowcapped River*, and one, to which he gave the enigmatic title *New York*, that was devoted to a typical summer traffic jam in the city.

The strong-willed Rockwell Kent, whose capacity for sustained rage against the art establishment (as represented by the leadership of the National Academy of Design) was greater than that of most of his rebellious colleagues, organized in March a second exhibition of the work of independent artists. But he stipulated that any painter who participated in *his* show must withhold all work from any Academy function. This provision, from which Kent couldn't be discouraged, produced a schism within the ranks of the younger artists, especially "The Eight," who had maintained for so long so solid a front. Arthur B. Davies, George Luks, and Maurice Prendergast agreed to abide by Kent's ruling; the remaining five refused. And George Bellows, associating himself completely with Robert Henri's assertion that exclusivity (no matter how laudable the intention) could be of no possible benefit to art or artists, refused to follow Kent's lead.

In spite of the important abstentions, the list of those who exhibited their work in "Kent's Tent," as the derisive art commentators of the day called it, makes impressive reading. In addition to those noted already, he was joined by John Marin (considered by Jackson Pollock and other abstract-expressionist painters of the fifties to be the most prophetic of American painters of the first half of this century), Alfred Henry Maurer, and Marsden Hartley. The rift between the two factions thus created was, alas, never entirely healed.

But George Bellows was not one to brood for very long about circumstances he was helpless to alter. Besides, there were many distractions. A traveling exhibition of contemporary painting that included examples of his work was seen in Detroit. One of the pictures shown there, *Up the River*, was purchased by Hugo Reisinger for three hundred dollars, less than the price Bellows had originally asked for it, but one that he had eagerly agreed to because of Reisinger's promise to make a gift of it immediately to the Metropolitan Museum of Art, considered the country's finest—which made of Bellows one of the youngest living painters ever to be represented there. When the same exhibition reached Chicago, Bellows' contributions to it were well received in the press, but no more were purchased.

The press didn't treat him with universal adulation in the course of that spring of 1911. The New York *Times*, which was then far from being the definitive newspaper it has since become, took him severely to task for depicting his adopted city as such a dreary place. His paintings, the *Times* critic said, were unfair to New York—by which, presumably, he meant that the city had features more attractive than excavation sites, a grubby waterfront, and shabby slums. He chose to take no notice of George's paintings, for example, of Central Park, the Battery, and Coney Island.

In this respect, the *Times* was at odds not only with the artist but with William Gaynor, the only good, honest, concerned mayor New York would have until the election of Fiorello La Guardia in 1933. Gaynor and Bellows saw their city in much the same light. There is no record of their having met, and though Gaynor was far from sympathetic with most of the political and economic ideas advanced by socialists and anarchists of the era, he readily agreed with them that the ghettos and slums of New York were an atrocity. He did not, unhappily, live long enough to alter them—but he meant to.

As if to show that official and popular recognition, even when cordially granted, could be a capricious thing, the directors of the Carnegie Institute in Pittsburgh rejected that spring all the paintings George had submitted for their exhibition. But as the summer approached, he could count the high art season of 1911 a success unparalleled in his career.

With Emma in the advanced stages of pregnancy, it was impossible for the couple to travel very far that summer. As housework became more difficult for his wife, and as the heat of the city became increasingly difficult to bear, George decided that the wisest move would be to the

Story house in Upper Montclair. The painter, unable to work in the crowded house, and suffering from a combination of the heat and the boredom that resulted from overexposure to suburban life, left his wife in the middle of July to join Robert and Marjorie Henri on Monhegan Island, Maine, the remote resort whose virtues Rockwell Kent had so loudly sung to them several years earlier.

George and Emma wrote to each other every day. She didn't reproach him for his departure, which isn't to suggest that she didn't feel sorry for herself, resentful over a pregnancy that she feared and for which he was responsible. She rarely failed to remind him of her apprehension and discomfort. The artist profited astonishingly from the six weeks he spent in Maine, and accomplished true prodigies of work—thirty small panels and twelve larger canvases, all devoted to scenes of Monhegan village and the surrounding sea. He returned to Upper Montclair around September 1, exactly a week before the birth of the baby to whom he and Emma had constantly referred during her pregnancy as "John"—for like so many fathers, George Bellows hoped for a son. "John" was born September 8, and it was clear at once that another name had to be selected. The parents named the infant Anne, for George's mother.

At the very beginning, the presence of a baby daughter in the Bellows household proved something of an encumbrance to parents accustomed to doing as they pleased, when they pleased. Few artists of record have made ideal fathers, in spite of the fact that many of them do their work at or near home. Indeed, their presence is as often a liability as an asset, because even when they are actually in the house, they are (so to speak) out of this world. Their thoughts, their preoccupations, are elsewhere—on their work—with the result that, except in the most dire of emergencies, they are infuriating for their powers to concentrate on their projects to the exclusion of everything going on about them. The other side of the coin, of course, is that, were this concentration not so absolute, artists would have to do their work somewhere else.

With the Bellowses as parents, little Anne quickly learned to adjust herself to the eccentricities of two intelligent, willful people who never hesitated to say to each other precisely what they thought—in terms that could be easily understood. George and Emma were more temperamental than querulous, and so far as their daughter was concerned, they usually more than compensated for occasional outbursts of hot feeling with expressions of warmth or love that were more tender.

As soon as the little family was reinstalled in Nineteenth Street, George set about painting again, mostly from his memories of his holiday in Maine—*Evening Swell, The Sea, Rich Woods, Three Rollers,* in all of which he showed the influence of his new friend, Leon Kroll, who was a disciple of the Impressionists. George's palette in these canvases was a great deal brighter and stronger than was usual for him. But, by November, his impulse to paint had ebbed considerably, and he was relieved to have other distractions to turn to.

Everett Shinn, who lived in nearby Waverly Place, had organized a theater in his back yard there, where he was producing, only for his friends at first, parodies of the horrendous melodramas that were the staple fare staged by touring companies throughout rural America. Of these plays, *East Lynne* is probably the best known, one that is hardly read today, and even less often seen. George lent a willing hand with the design and manufacture of the sets; Emma provided the incidental music. To the surprise of everyone connected with these amateur theatricals, they soon drew the attention of members of the New York press corps. Critics attending some of the performances were delighted by the charm and wit of these talented people.

By the end of the year, George was able to return to his work feeling altogether refreshed by his brief excursion into the theater. He painted several pictures of scenes like those he had done several times before—*Snow Dumpers, Winter Road,* and a new rendition of *Men of the Docks.* He submitted this last painting, when its protective coat of varnish was scarcely dry, for the spring exhibition of the National Academy of Design. James Huneker, who was fancied by many (himself included) to have the highest brow of all the city's critics of art and literature—and who was an intimate friend of John Quinn, a connoisseur and major collector of contemporary art and manuscript material—heaped vast scorn on *Men of the Docks.* To add insult to injury, Huneker accused Bellows of having neither social consciousness nor a true political outlook.

This allegation, made out of an ignorance of which Huneker was a gifted master, offended the artist far more than the denigration of a particular work of art. For the fact was that Bellows had never been more politically involved, personally and artistically, than he was in 1912. He was a frequent contributor of drawings to *The Masses,* a radical monthly of which his friend John Sloan was art editor (and of which Max Eastman, later to wash himself clean of his youthful radicalism in *The Reader's Digest,* was editor-in-chief). In the shabby offices of *The Masses,* George made the acquaintance of John Reed, whose *Ten Days that Shook the World,* published almost a decade later, would give the English-speaking peoples a vivid, if highly romanticized, description of the November 1917 revolution in Russia.

A strange aspect of Huneker's criticism of Bellows' painting was his comparison of the artist's imagery with the poetry of Walt Whitman, whose work the painter first encountered at Ohio State. Given the view, popular in 1912, that Whitman had been not only a decadent but a radical poet, it seemed that the critic was unable to make up his mind about George. Even more extraordinary was a published report on Bellows by Robert McIntyre, nephew of the gallery owner William Macbeth who had given "The Eight" their first public showing in New York. McIntyre likened Bellows to Rudyard Kipling. The pitiable poverty of mind that afflicted the art critics of 1912, like the poverty of the slums, is with us today. Tastes have changed, but writers on art have found no more-imaginative ways of saying that they admire or despise or are utterly indifferent to the work they are required to write about. *Men of the Docks,* which Huneker so disliked in 1912, was to receive a year later the Sesnan Award of the Pennsylvania Academy of Fine Arts.

In February 1912, a group of younger artists, including some names that would become familiar with the passage of the years, including Walt Kuhn, Jerome Myers, and Elmer MacRae, gathered in New York to discuss the formation of an organization that would be called the Association of American Painters and Sculptors. The purpose of this new group was to arrange for the following year an exhibition, similar in spirit to Robert Henri's Independent Show and Kent's Tent—though from the latter it would differ in that it would exclude no artist who wished to participate. Arthur B. Davies was elected president, with the sculptor Gutzon Borglum (who would later adorn the side of Mount Rushmore, South Dakota, with the portrait-busts of great Americans) as vice-president.

Davies agreed to serve in this newly created post provided that the show would include examples of European painting and sculpture of the present and the recent past. It is painful to have to record that, had the committee been even vaguely aware of just what Davies had in mind, its members would surely have rejected his demand. For the exhibition of American art that he and Walt Kuhn supplemented with European was to be known to posterity as the Armory Show of 1913, an event that simply transfigured the world of American painting and sculpture. Yet, at the time, the request seemed a reasonable one, and the committee readily assented to it, relieved to find in Davies one who was willing to give so much of his time and energy to what everyone agreed was a noble cause—contemporary art. As we shall see, Davies set about to bite off a great deal more than most of his fellows were willing to chew.

During this spring of 1912 Bellows created summer scenes—*Luncheon in the Park*, a drawing that was to serve as inspiration for a later painting, *A Day in June*. At this time, too, he made *Splinter Beach*, based on sketches he had drawn the previous summer at Monhegan Island. In addition to the drawings he provided at no charge to *The Masses*, he sold a series of illustrations for one hundred fifty dollars to *Collier's*, and before the year was out had realized one thousand dollars for this kind of work—his first ventures into this lucrative field.

To many Americans, April 1912 was made memorable by the sinking of the "unsinkable" *Titanic* on her maiden voyage from Liverpool. To the radicals of this country, however, that tragedy was almost wholly eclipsed by the spectacular strike against the textile mills of Lawrence, Massachusetts, which was marked by serious outbreaks of violence. This industrial dispute had been instigated by the Industrial Workers of the World under the leadership of Big Bill Haywood, whose advocacy of a policy of total war against the propertied class had produced a crisis within the governing body of the Socialist party. The executive committee, presided over by Eugene Debs, expelled Haywood from membership because of his insistence on violent tactics. He remained, however, chief of the IWW and, the following year, led a similarly violent and successful strike against the firm of Cluett, Peabody, in Paterson, New Jersey.

Bellows found himself very much of two minds about Haywood, whom he met for the first time in the spring of 1912 at the house of Robert Henri. Though he was sympathetic with anarchist philosophy, as we have already observed, he drew the line against violence, and was unable to reconcile this confusion in his mind. Haywood as an individual impressed Bellows very much, however much he disapproved of the labor leader's proclamation of "class warfare." He could easily appreciate the comment made by the prominent British labor politician Ramsay MacDonald, who described Haywood as "a bundle of primitive instincts— a torch amongst a crowd of uncritical, credulous workingmen." It seems a pity that Bellows never portrayed Haywood, whom he never saw again. When the United States entered World War I, the anarchist was arrested on a charge of sedition for his opposition to our participation in a conflict from which Russia—soon to be the Soviet Union—had only recently retired. Released on bail, Haywood fled to Moscow in 1918 and died there a decade later.

To what degree Bellows was influenced by the politics of Haywood and his comrades we may only speculate. It may have had some effect on his decision to try to put art at the disposal of a much larger number of people than had hitherto been possible. But the inspiration seems to have come more directly from Cornell University's invitation to send some of his work for a show at Ithaca. George agreed without hesitation, and then proposed a series of exhibitions that were to travel from college to college throughout the country, his idea being to try to improve the quality of art instruction on university campuses—bearing in mind, no doubt, the dismally miserable courses available to him at Ohio State years before. He believed that only one institution could be said to escape this blanket condemnation, Harvard, whose professor of the history of art, Charles Eliot Norton, provided excellent instruction and facilities for his pupils. In planning these traveling shows, he was in frequent correspondence with Joe Taylor in Columbus, who was naturally in full agreement with Bellows—but in the end, nothing seems to have come of the plan.

With summer coming on, there was a brisk debate in the Bellows household about where to spend the holidays. Emma was reluctant to go to a shore resort, because she feared that the infant Anne, who could crawl now with a rapidity that was rather frightening, might slip away from her on the beach and be drowned. In addition, it appears that the young mother was weary of having total responsibility for her daughter, and looked for some relief during the summer. So she and George decided to spend the hottest months once again with the Storys in Upper Montclair—a choice that was made all the more definite when Bellows learned from his mother that Ben Monett, his half sister Laura's husband, was dying in Columbus; so he must be ready at any time to make the journey home.

The alumni association of Ohio State University commissioned the artist in late June to paint the portrait of retiring professor Walter Quincy Scott, for which he received three hundred dollars—the largest sum he had yet received for this kind of picture. But money remained in very short supply as the family made the short trip from New York to Upper Montclair. With her mother left to look after little Anne, Emma devoted much of her vacation to the organization and presentation of a "society circus," whose festive spirit reminded George of the traveling carnivals that had come to Columbus during his boyhood. In this frame of mind, he made two paintings of the event, *Outside the Big Tent* and *Circus,* both crowd scenes, of which he was very much a master.

The long-forecast death of Ben Monett propelled the artist to Columbus in August. He had been fond of his brother-in-law, though the two men had had very little in common. He was, therefore, surprised and moved to learn that he had been left one thousand dollars in Ben's will—enough, as George wrote Emma at once, to pay all their debts; they could face the autumn with a lot more peace of mind than they had anticipated. On his return to New Jersey, he and his wife gratefully accepted the invitation of the Haggins to spend some time with them at Onteora, in the Catskills, where there was more time for relaxation than for work.

During this summer that was not very entertaining for the Bellowses, Arthur B. Davies and Walt Kuhn were in Europe gathering paintings and sculptures to display in the exhibition that was scheduled to open in New York the following February. No one in America had the remotest notion of what the two men were up to abroad; the rumors that drifted back were too extraordinary to be believed—that they were collecting literally hundreds of works for the occasion.

The Sunday magazine of the New York *Herald* published in the late summer an illustrated interview with George Bellows in which his talents as a painter of the people were richly praised. He was quoted significantly: "I can't see anything in the worship of beauty which some people seek to develop. Beauty is easy to paint; just as easy as something grotesque. What really counts is interest." In 1912 George was saying more or less exactly what Robert Henri had said eight years before. And we have only to go back to Bellows' work to see where his interest lay— in people, in their loneliness (as in crowds), and in his own loneliness (as in his landscapes and seascapes, of which his production increased from year to year).

In October, when Anne Bellows was just a little more than a year old, her father painted his first picture of her— *My Baby*. This subject, his own children and others, was the last major theme that Bellows introduced into his repertory. He might not be the earth's best father, but he was certainly filled with love for his daughter, and this affection flooded the first small canvas as it would all the paintings and sketches and lithographs that he made of his two daughters.

The controversial success of the exhibition given to him and to members of "The Eight" by the Carnegie Library in Columbus eighteen months or so earlier prompted the art committee of that institution to invite Bellows to put on a one-man show in November of 1912. He and Emma attended the opening. The notices accorded the occasion were universally enthusiastic, and there is no doubt that the painter was delighted by the ovation given him in his home town. He and Emma remained in Columbus for more than a month, over the Christmas holiday. The Pen and Pencil Club gave him a room in which to work, and he lectured often to pupils of the newly established Columbus School of Art—mainly on Maratta's theories of color. He had, as well, the pleasure of painting the portrait of his old friend Joe Taylor, and the even greater joy of giving the picture to him as a Christmas present. But certainly the most gratifying part of his success in Columbus that winter was the pride it inspired in his father, who, at eighty-five, was described once again as "failing."

When the exhibition moved from Columbus to Toledo and then to Detroit (where it was less warmly received), George and Emma returned to New York. By this time, in January 1913, a terrific storm was beginning to brew over the impending opening of the International Art Exhibition that was to occupy the Armory of the 69th Infantry Regiment (the "Fighting Sixty-ninth"), at Lexington Avenue and Twenty-fifth Street. The cause of the row was simple enough: Davies and Kuhn had, as the rumors of the summer had indicated, accumulated what most members of the committee thought as an unconscionably large quantity of foreign works for the show. Yet Davies had been given a free hand, and at this point, only a few weeks before the doors were to open, there seemed no course but to proceed as he had planned.

On February 5, Gutzon Borglum resigned his post as vice-president of the committee, which, in any event, he had occupied in name only; Davies and Kuhn had assumed the direction of the project. On the tenth, only five days before the exhibition was to open, the Armory was made available to the organizers. The amount of work to be done in the intervening time was colossal—décor, lighting, the construction and placement of panels on which pictures were to be hung, not to mention the actual arrangement of the eighteen hundred individual items, domestic and foreign, that had been submitted. To this enormous undertaking, all the members of the committee, not least the very handy George Bellows, contributed a labor of love.

By the evening·of February 14, all was in comparative readiness for the press preview. There had already been a considerable amount of advance publicity for the exhibition, generated by Borglum's abrupt resignation and the ensuing exchange of charges. The exhibition itself provided topics for much lively newspaper copy. The major subject of journalistic discussion was *Nude Descending a Staircase,* by Marcel Duchamps, that French painter's revolutionary attempt to capture a sense of motion within a static framework.

But contrary to the legend that has developed over the years since 1913, the Armory Show did *not* produce in the press generally a response that could be called hostile. What appears to have occurred in the retelling is that the fairly universal reaction to the Duchamps painting has been attributed to what was said of the exhibition as a whole—and this was just not the case. Of far greater consequence in the longer term was the quantity of painting and drawings by Cézanne, Gauguin, and Van Gogh on display; their exposure in New York, and later on in the show's tour of Boston and Chicago, had a profound effect on the tastes of American collectors and, understandably, on the styles of American painters.

The Armory Show was certainly something of a milestone (and to some, a millstone). It has been common to say that art in America was never the same afterward, by which it is implied that our artists were immediately revolutionized. This appears not to be so. True, some painters (Bellows not among them) were profoundly changed by their opportunity to view something like four hundred European works (most of them French), but there is no reason to suppose that the transformations that took place over the next generations would not have happened had there been nothing like the Armory Show. Few were the American artists and collectors who didn't manage to make at least one prolonged visit to Paris, where,

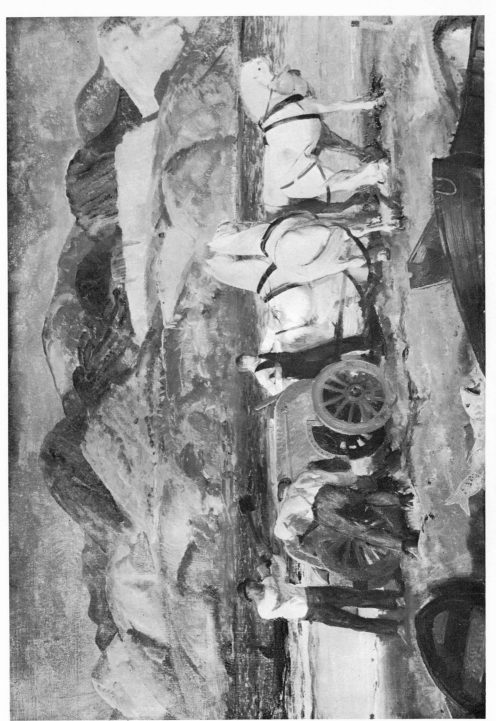

19) THE SAND TEAM, 1917. In The Brooklyn Museum Collection.

20) EDITH CAVELL, 1918. Springfield Museum of Fine Arts, Springfield, Massachusetts, The James Philip Gray Collection.

21) FOOTBALL, 1918. Courtesy H. V. Allison & Company, Inc., Collection of Mr. Albert L. Sylvester.

22) EMMA IN BLACK PRINT, 1919. Courtesy, Museum of Fine Arts, Boston, Bequest of John T. Spaulding.

23) TENNIS AT NEWPORT, 1919. The Metropolitan Museum of Art,
Bequest of Miss Adelaide Milton de Groot (1876-1967), 1967.

24) ELINOR, JEAN AND ANNA, 1920. Albright-Knox Art Gallery, Buffalo, New York, Charles Clifton Fund.

25) JEAN, 1920. Albright-Knox Art Gallery, Buffalo, New York, A. Conger Goodyear Collection.

26) AUNT FANNY, 1920. Des Moines Art Center, James D. Edmundson Fund.

27) ANNE IN WHITE, 1920. Museum of Art, Carnegie Institute, Pittsburgh, Pennsylvania.

28) THE WHITE HORSE, 1921. Worcester Art Museum.

29) PORTRAIT OF MY MOTHER, 1921. The Columbus Gallery of
Fine Arts, Columbus, Ohio: Gift of Emma S. Bellows.

30) INTRODUCING JOHN L. SULLIVAN, 1923. From the Collection
of Mr. and Mrs. John Hay Whitney.

31) EMMA AND HER CHILDREN, 1923. Courtesy, Museum of Fine Arts, Boston, Gift of Subscribers and the John Lowell Gardner Fund.

32) DEMPSEY AND FIRPO, 1924. Collection Whitney Museum of American Art, New York.

33) LADY JEAN, 1924. Yale University Art Gallery, Bequest
of Stephen Carlton Clark, B.A., 1903.

34) RINGSIDE SEATS, 1924. Courtesy of the Fogg Art Museum, Harvard University, Grenville L. Winthrop Bequest. Photo: Courtesy of H. V. Allison & Company, Inc., New York.

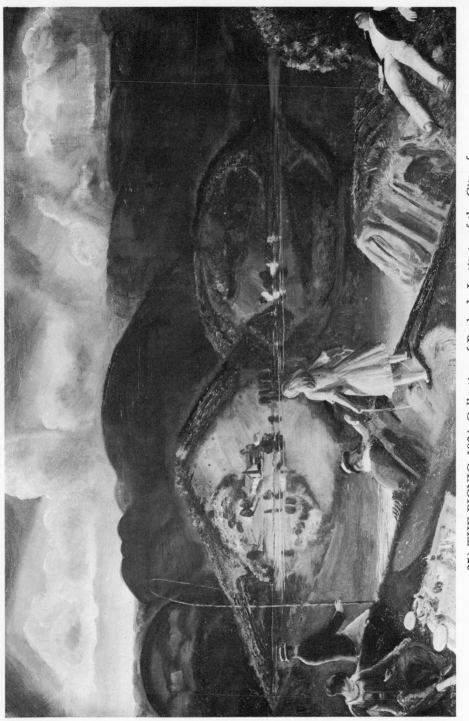

35) THE PICNIC, 1924. Collection of Peabody Institute of the City of Baltimore, George C. Irwin Fund.

as the phrase now is, it was all happening. However, the impact of the show on the ninety thousand-odd New Yorkers who attended during its month's run is more difficult (if not impossible) to measure.

In financial terms, the Armory Show was a distinctly losing proposition. The largest private purchaser was John Quinn, who invested a little less than six thousand dollars —surpassed only by the Metropolitan Museum of Art, which paid sixty-seven hundred dollars for the first work of Cézanne's to be bought by an American institution. In all three cities where the exhibition made a visit, a total of only about forty-four thousand dollars was realized from sales. And during the first fortnight of its stay in New York, it seemed that it would be a failure, too, from the standpoint of attendance. Apart from a number of artists who daily haunted its cavernous precincts, it was, again, John Quinn who was most conspicuously in evidence, almost every day—and especially so when he was seen escorting the former President of the United States, Teddy Roosevelt, around the vast hall. Roosevelt, who had just been defeated in his attempt to be re-elected President on the third-party Bull Moose ticket, didn't know quite how to respond to the strange-looking objects that the prominent New York lawyer and collector pointed out to him. His comment, we gather, was invariable: "Bully," he said.

At the beginning of March, for no evident reason, attendance suddenly picked up, averaging well over five thousand per day for the final two weeks. It was the crowds that attracted the attention of the cartoonists; and the cartoons that appeared in the newspapers, in turn, attracted more crowds. The high-quality art monthly *Art and Decoration* elicited from John Quinn, who turned out to be the angel of the Armory Show, the observation "Life is growth; stagnation, the failure to grow, is the great tragedy of art." For all his support of this exhibition, Quinn was not a notable patron of American art. Aside from a subscription to the full run of John Sloan's etchings, Quinn confined himself to purchases of work by Davies, Ernest Lawson, and Walt Kuhn. He was an acquaintance of Robert Henri's and had almost certainly encountered Bellows more than once, but he was never to buy a picture of George's.

Fortunately for the young father, he was never dependent on any single patron for his success. He did sell a few works out of the Armory Show, but by the time it left New York his mind was on other matters. He had been asked to take part in the judging of the National Academy of Design exhibition that would soon open. And hardly was this task completed when he learned that his father had died in Columbus of "senility." He hastened home for the funeral. Anna Bellows was philosophical in her bereavement, the more so, perhaps, because life for her during the past few months with the aged invalid had been very trying. Moreover, she was well provided for—a great relief to her son, who was in no position to support his mother, since it was becoming too plain that he would soon be called upon to give financial aid to Emma's parents.

The Later Years to World War I

In a summary that reflects his capacity to be honest and objective about his own feelings, George Bellows wrote this of his father shortly after his death: "He was a wonderfully fine man, and yet having been born in 1827, and being fifty-five when I appeared, his point of view, his character even, belonged to so remote a past that I look upon many of his ideas to this day with amazement and sorrow. Certain things he could not discuss. On religion, the church, and respect for the law he was above reproach."

Yet we may easily guess that it was the "certain things he could not discuss," as well as matters of religion and respect for the law, that the son would most have liked to iron out with his father—the very subjects upon which agreement between them was out of the question. A less charitable child would very likely have broken with a parent over issues so fundamental; a less charitable father would very likely have broken with the son for the same reasons. It was a high compliment to their mutual forbearance that they could love each other in spite of their grave differences of opinion and what we now call "life style."

When George returned from his father's funeral in Columbus, he encountered a minor scandal. The painting of about five years earlier, *Little Girl in White,* that he had submitted for the National Academy of Design exhibition, was given the Hallgarten first prize of three hundred dollars—in spite of the mixed notices it had received in the press. Since the artist had been a member of the jury that had selected all the exhibits, there were inevitable cries of favoritism. These were especially galling to Emma, who was still unaccustomed to the rough-and-tumble of politics in the world of art, but George took it all philosophically as a portion of the price of recognition. He accepted the prize money and ignored the scorn.

When the International Exhibition had completed its last stand in Chicago, Arthur B. Davies convened a meeting of the original organizing committee to announce that there was a rather large deficit, which had somehow to be made up. It is highly probable, given his vitriolic tongue and forceful opinions, that Davies didn't express himself with a maximum of tact, especially in view of his highhanded tactics in assembling (at so great an expense) so many foreign works for this show. In response to his request for material and/or moral assistance in financing the debt, the entire membership of the committee resigned—Robert Henri, Guy Pène duBois, Mahonri Young, and George Bellows among them. Only Walt Kuhn stood by his friend Davies in his hour of need, and together (with the financial and influential assistance of the connoisseur John Quinn) they raised the required sum of money. In retrospect, we must regard the action of Henri and Bellows and the others as both churlish and rather childish. The Armory Show was a watershed in the history of American art, and even if, as was the case with Bellows, it was to have only a minor effect, its impact must have been plainly important from the evening it opened its doors to the press on February 14, 1913.

There is a marked difference of opinion among Bellows specialists about the ultimate effect of the Armory on the painter's work. One authority states flatly that it so shook Bellows that he never quite regained his nerve as an artist and that his work over the remaining eleven years of his life was timid—mere restatements of positions (theoretically speaking) he had taken before in his art. Another writer, Charles H. Morgan, author of the only full-length biography of Bellows, suggests that the Armory Show strengthened the painter and headed him in new directions.

It appears to the writer of the book in hand that there was no immediate change in Bellows' work in the wake of the International Exhibition—in terms either of technique or of thematic material. Bellows frequently spoke with a special warmth about Marcel Duchamp's highly controversial canvas *Nude Descending a Staircase,* but he always had a doubt in his mind about Duchamp's sincerity of purpose in this work—felt that it might be some sort of terrible (though fascinating) joke.

Herein, one is permitted to believe, may lie the key to Bellows' view of the entire Armory Show, his first and only comprehensive view of a whole range of contemporary European art. He respected it without having the slightest desire to emulate it. The painting that he did in the months and years after the exhibition's departure from New York did reflect some changes; but as we shall see, it was not so much the work displayed in the Armory Show that changed him as it was the ideas of Jay Hambidge, father of a theory of painting he called "Dynamic Symmetry."

The day-to-day work of the artist continued. He was pleased to learn, later in the spring, that the Carnegie Institute in Pittsburgh had awarded a third prize to his painting *The Circus.* He would certainly have preferred first prize, but any award was better than none at all; and the judges did spell his name correctly. He must have enjoyed very mixed emotions about the next accolade to come his way, the announcement by the members of the National Academy of Design that he had been elected a full member. However violently he continued to disapprove of the Academy's policies with regard to contemporary art, he doubtless felt, as had Robert Henri before him, that it was better to work for an improvement of official academic taste within the organization than to remain half in and half out (the position of associate member), excluded from any hand in formulating policy, but vilified, as he had been in the spring, for acts of the Academy in which he had had no part. And finally, it is relevant to remind ourselves that in 1913, *not* to be an academician could be a severe drawback to the professional painter. We need look no further than the career of John Sloan to observe the result. Though ten years Bellows' senior, he was still surviving largely through the sale of his etchings; hardly a Sloan canvas was sold until long after George Bellows' death. Again, we have no records to suggest why the academicians decided to elect the Ohioan to full membership. Conjecture is not helpful.

For *The Masses,* in May, George contributed a drawing of the poor who swarmed the streets of New York during the summer months, to which he gave the bitter title *Why Don't They All Go to the Country for Vacation?* Later on, he elaborated on this theme in a painting that became briefly popular, *The Cliff Dwellers.* In the next month he completed two pictures, *A Day in June* (for which, as we've noted, he had made studies earlier) and *Approach to the Bridge, Night,* yet another treatment of the recently finished Queensborough Bridge.

When Robert and Marjorie Henri departed late in June

for Ireland (apparently persuaded by John Quinn and John Butler Yeats, the aged Irish portraitist living in New York, that there lay in that soft little country a new source of inspiration for his work), the Bellowses went to Monhegan Island, Maine, where they found the bachelor Leon Kroll already established for the vacation months. Kroll encouraged George to add stronger, more-brilliant colors to his palette; and no doubt the dazzling work of the young French painters, known collectively as *Les Fauves* (the wild beasts), was influential, too. In these brighter hues, the artist painted seascapes—*Island in the Sea, Rock-Bound,* and *Cream Surf.* He made the seven-mile voyage to lonely Matinicus Isle with its single, tiny fishing village, Criehaven, which became a frequent subject of his painting that summer and thereafter.

The Bellowses remained in Maine through October, during which time George painted forty-two pictures, many of them quite large. By the time they left for New York, he was exhausted. Early in the new year, still fatigued and still smoking much more than was good for him (he drank almost nothing by way of wine or beer or spirits), and wearied of drawing on his storehouse of recollections of Monhegan and Matinicus for his pictures, he wrote at length to Joe Taylor in Columbus: ". . . I have come to the realization that permanence demands more care, and while I am certain that my pictures are as 'stable' as any modern technic [sic], I also realize that there are grave dangers in too much spontaneity and haste.

"I am glad that most of my good pictures have been on new, mostly white canvas, and that I use permanent colors and good mediums. But the Old Masters got different results and I want to know how they did it. . . . I expect to change my methods entirely when I learn what I can in a new direction, that direction being the isolation of drawing and coloring into two distinct processes and over a perfectly prepared canvas of pure white. This is the process of Rubens, Titian, Velasquez, Hals and the rest. . . .

"This seems to be an extremely original attitude nowadays. All this is very hopeful, of course, and I am not beyond hope."

It is obvious that something more overwhelming than temporary weariness was at the root of these words. And we need not read too much into so doleful a letter to conclude that the artist was in a state of doubt about the value of his own old methods of painting what came naturally to him. The fact is that during the summer he had been experimenting with Hardesty Maratta's new "triad" theory of using colors on a canvas. He was also influenced in this period by the artistic philosophy of Professor Denman Ross, of Harvard, whose book *On Drawing and Painting* referred to "color unlimited," and a means of denoting the motions of the body that Bellows found intriguing— though he disagreed with Ross' disapproval of the Post-Impressionist painters in general and Duchamp's *Nude Descending a Staircase* in particular.

We may idly speculate on the advisability of Bellows' tinkering with theory and method at this advanced stage of a successful career. He was hardly the first artist to wonder if he was on the right track, however smoothly the train seemed to be running. The problems of painting with which he was so suddenly coming to grips were more or less involved with an attempt to reconcile two schools of artistic thought that had been at odds since the High Renaissance—the draftsmen and the colorists. One might imagine that with the centuries already piled so high, such a dispute would have been resolved by the first months of 1914. In fact, it *had* been resolved definitively by the Impressionists, who had simply discarded all pre-

viously accepted platitudes about the value of drawing and
line and given themselves up completely to the infinite
possibilities that lay before them in the application of
color. But what was true for Paris was far from being
true for New York just a year after the Armory Show. The
question was not academic in America, and it would be
a full generation before it would even approach this stage
of dry, empty debate.

Bellows was never to resolve the question to his own
satisfaction, but the very fact that he was involved in such
an inquiry, as his letter to Joe Taylor and his summer
reading and experiment indicate, reveals the extent to
which he was conscious of a difficulty. He continued to
torment himself occasionally about method for the rest
of his life, and there are those who believe that his attempts to alter his approach to art were not very successful.
We can, however, only respect a craftsman who seeks, no
matter how misguidedly, to improve himself, and may well
ponder the result of such attempts had Bellows been given
the time to develop them to a fuller maturity.

A month or two after writing to Taylor, George drew
a picture of a scene he had beheld both in Columbus
and, more frequently, in New York—hobos exploring the
contents of garbage cans. The title he gave this study was
Disappointments of the Ash Can. Since this little work is
a comparative unknown in the large body of work that
Bellows left behind on his death, it is extremely doubtful
that the title had any bearing at all on the later designation
"The Ashcan School," which was ascribed to the group of
which George and Sloan and Glackens were the acknowledged masters. The origins of the description are, as the
saying is, lost in the mists of history—though it appears
first to have been pronounced after 1930 and was not in-

tended to be flattering to those it covered, the early social-realist painters.

Not since his days as a student at Ohio State had George made any drawings of the game he still occasionally played and that was his and the country's favorite at the time, baseball. He sketched two versions of *The National Sport* in the winter of 1914. If he made any other baseball studies during the last ten years of his life, they were of little significance. As a counterbalance to these little drawings that he did apparently for his own amusement, he made a sketch of a prayer meeting based on his casual attendance at an evening service at Monhegan the previous summer. And he wrote Joe Taylor, in this connection, that he regretted having missed a performance of Billy Sunday, the sensationally successful evangelist who enjoyed a popularity not again equaled until the epoch of Billy Graham. It seems not the case that Bellows was seeking a new avenue to religion, but rather that he was fascinated by all kinds of public spectacles, and the reports of Billy Sunday's revival meetings suggested the sort of great gathering of people that the artist liked to witness and depict.

In February, just before the opening of a second one-man show at the fashionable Montross Gallery, Bellows painted *Love of Winter,* whose vivid colors disclose the lessons he had absorbed from the writings of Ross and Maratta and the advice of Leon Kroll. The Montross show, where he exhibited two dozen pictures (nineteen of them from the group painted at Monhegan), was not a great financial success. The major work sold was *Palisades* (a view across the Hudson from upper Manhattan that he had painted in 1909), for which he received only six hundred dollars. And neither of the paintings he submitted to the exhibition of the Pennsylvania Academy of Fine Arts that spring, *Polo Crowd* and *Cliff Dwellers,* was purchased.

There was some consolation, however, this season. A portrait of Dr. William Oxley Thompson, former president of Ohio State, that George had painted a couple of years before, was awarded the Maynard prize for portraiture at the National Academy of Design show in New York; and in Pittsburgh, the jury of the Carnegie Institute bestowed yet another third prize on a Bellows work, *Cliff Dwellers*. But the principal achievement of the spring, from the standpoint of the Bellows family finances, was the commission to portray the rich businessman Willard Straight, a relative by marriage of the artist's friend Gertrude Vanderbilt Whitney, who happily remitted the enormous sum of fifteen hundred dollars for the work, by far the highest price George had ever received for a single picture.

Emma, George, and three-year-old Anne returned for the summer to Monhegan, and this year the painter worked more boldly with color, using what Denman Ross referred to as a "Rubens palette," which, as a matter of fact, was much more a Maratta palette. Of the many pictures he accomplished during this holiday, the finest were of those nearest and dearest to him—*Family Group* and *Emma at the Piano,* both moving for their expression of love.

The Bellowses were with a few of their painter friends at Monhegan in July of 1914 when they learned that the long-expected war between the members of the Triple Alliance and those of the Triple Entente had broken out in Europe. Like most Americans, not excepting President Woodrow Wilson, they were both dismayed by this development and anxious that the United States remain aloof from the distant conflict. Sympathies in the country generally were not nearly so firmly on the side of Britain, France, and Imperial Russia as we now believe. A high proportion of the nation was genuinely neutral, and the large minority that constituted the Irish-American community was willing to support Germany in order to free Ireland from the British yoke. With a few exceptions, German-Americans kept their feelings to themselves—which was just as well, because when America did become involved directly in the war, there was a hysterical reaction against all things German that can be compared only with the similar and disgraceful behavior of the government and people toward native Americans of Japanese descent after Pearl Harbor.

On the whole, however, the war in Europe meant little to most Americans until the winter of 1917. Except for a few weeks in August and early September of 1914, when the Germans very nearly gained a stunning victory (as in fact they did in the spring of 1940) before the French were prepared to fight, it was a war that excited no one's fancy. Such heroics as there were seemed confined to the novelty of aerial dogfights. On the ground, where France would lose in dead alone a million and a half of her young men, there was no glamour at all, for there was very little movement in either direction. The two great armies fought battles that lasted as long as six months without moving more than ten miles to east or west; or at least such was the case on the Western Front in France and Belgium.

When George Bellows and his little family reached New York in the autumn, he was pleased to find further interest in portraits by his hand. To offset the proceeds from this new market, the William Storys, whose fortunes had been steadily in decline, became almost entirely his responsibility. They moved into an apartment of the Bellows house in Nineteenth Street, where they remained for the rest of the artist's life. It is an eloquent commentary on his good nature and kindliness that there appears not a single record of prolonged resentment over this state of affairs on either side. There were, of necessity, occasional disagreements, for it would be hard to find two men more different in out-

look than William Story and his son-in-law. But as Bellows
had written of his dead father, so too could he say of
Story—that he was above reproach. The new situation required tact and delicacy, and it is plain that these qualities
were exercised with generosity.

Of the artists who constituted what was to be called
"The Ashcan School," Bellows alone was able at this time
to market the pictures he felt like painting. We have always remarked on Sloan's inability to dispose of *his* canvases. William Glackens' greatest period of recognition followed George's death. Only in portraiture was he rivaled,
and the explanation seems inescapable: Bellows was at his
best when composing pictures he wanted to paint. His
portraits failed when the subjects were, for whatever reasons, unsympathetic to him. Consequently, few Bellows
portraits of people who were comparative or total strangers
to him are convincing. Conversely, few portraitists so well
and warmly expressed in their pictures their feelings for
subjects they admired or loved. This is close to the essence
of Bellows' solid achievement as an artist; his enthusiasm
and verve and spontaneity are immediately apparent in his
good work, and their absence is equally evident in his indifferent pictures.

The wave of affluence and popularity that he was now
enjoying was reflected as well in other areas of his profession. He served on several major juries at the end of 1914
and the beginning of the following year. The most important
assignment was as a member of a committee to select work
to be exhibited at the Panama-Pacific Exposition in San
Francisco. Joining him on this jury was the veteran artist
J. Alden Weir, twenty years his senior, the premier American Impressionist of his day.

When George's painting *River Front* was awarded the
Gold Medal of the Panama-Pacific Exposition, his dear

friend and former master Robert Henri was put out, for the first time during their long acquaintance, because his own contribution received only an Honorable Mention. Though Bellows couldn't say it and certainly *wouldn't* say it, the award and what it signified were simple justice; he was and had been for some time a much better painter than Henri —a truth that took nothing from his friend's reputation as a teacher and tireless promoter of contemporary painting and sculpture.

New York's *Metropolitan Magazine* gave George the opportunity he had written Joe Taylor he wanted the year before—to see Billy Sunday in action. The editor of the publication dispatched him and the brilliant radical reporter John Reed to Philadelphia, where the fabled gospel-orator was drawing crowds in their thousands to an enormous circus tent and inducing a great proportion of each of his audiences to "hit the sawdust trail," declaring their faith in Christ's teachings as interpreted by the fanatical evangelist. Bellows was at once repelled and fascinated by Billy Sunday, whose religious bigotry and demagogy had so great an appeal to so many people. He held them quite literally spellbound. The sketches George made at the time and the lithographs he later created are evidence of his powerful dislike.

Back in New York in March, he painted the portrait of his acquaintance Paul Manship, one of the worst and most highly considered sculptors of his age—whose work would one day clutter the atrium of Rockefeller Center, where it is still to be seen in its gilded slickness. In fairness to Manship, however, this example of his public art is no worse than much sculpture of this kind. Bellows' portrait is very sympathetic, leading us to suppose him an admirer of the sculptor, if not of his sculpture.

The sale of two of the Monhegan paintings he had

exhibited the year before in the Montross Gallery occurred shortly before April 23, 1915, the date that Jean Bellows (named for the painter's great friend Eugene Speicher) was born. Jean's birth, greeted with commendable joy by a father who still would have liked to have a son, was much on his mind when he learned of the sinking of the British passenger vessel *Lusitania* by a German submarine just off the south coast of Ireland. Of 1153 lives lost in this tragedy, which had taken place without warning, 114 were Americans. Whatever sympathy there had been in the United States for the German cause in the war was largely dissipated by this event.

Many Americans who had long quietly advocated this nation's intervention in a war that seemed more and more to be stalemated, now began actively to campaign for such a move. Woodrow Wilson, rightly thinking this a minority viewpoint, settled for an unsatisfactory exchange of diplomatic messages that resulted in nothing more positive than the German promise to sink no more passenger ships. Nevertheless, the incident, though closed, was the first major step in the psychological preparation for America's entry on the Allied side.

Like virtually every socialist and anarchist, George Bellows thought the war a criminal undertaking between two sets of equally imperialistic powers, neither of them worth preservation. In the face of increasing pressure on all sides for America to take a position, militarily, in favor of the Triple Entente, he remained steadfast in his pacifism. With the provocation of the sinking of the *Lusitania*, this stand became more difficult—particularly on the eastern seaboard of the United States, where the war fever grew higher day by day.

As the father of two small children and the protector of his parents-in-law, George didn't allow himself to be long depressed by the state of the world. There was work to be done. There was, specifically, a portrait to be made of Judge Peter Olney, whose likeness, as retiring president of the Harvard Club of New York, was by tradition and right to hang in one of the public rooms of that establishment. Bellows liked the finished work as much as any commissioned portrait he had ever done, and it was with pride that he supervised its installation in the club just before he and his family departed for Ogunquit, Maine, where they would spend the summer. If George imagined that this was the last he would hear of this picture of Judge Olney (and he probably did), he was bitterly mistaken.

For the holiday season, however, all was tranquillity. In addition to Emma and the children and the Storys, Anna Bellows, the painter's mother, contributed her substantial bulk to the Maine scene, where the Henris and Leon Kroll were also summering. George's major efforts at Ogunquit were two nudes, the first he had painted in nearly a decade. The first, *Nude with a Parrot,* was subsequently purchased by Gertrude Vanderbilt Whitney. The second, *Torso of a Girl,* prompted an amusing comment from Anna Bellows, to whom nudity, even in the higher interest of art, was repugnant and scandalous: "It's bad enough, George, to paint a girl with both of her breasts bare, but to show only one is nasty."

Relations between Bellows and Robert Henri had not been wholly cordial since January, when George's painting had been awarded the Gold Medal of the Panama-Pacific Exposition. They were further strained that summer, when Henri expressed considerable (and not very comprehensible) anger over a charming portrait that Bellows had painted of Lucie Bayard, a teen-aged girl who was acting as permanent baby sitter for the Henris. This blight on a friendship that the younger man treasured was, fortunately, of very brief duration, but it didn't make his memories of the Ogunquit summer very happy. The Bellowses never returned there.

If the holidays were unhappy, worse was to come. After Labor Day, when the members of the Harvard Club reconvened in New York to talk with each other about the blessings of the life afforded the graduates of the university that adorns the bank of the river Charles, George learned to his astonishment and consternation that his portrait of Judge Peter Olney was the object of intense controversy. A majority of the club's members demanded that the work be completely repainted. Quite properly, Bellows refused. A painter of his stature, he asserted, was under no obligation to justify a style of portrait well known to any client before a commission was agreed to. The argument raged back and forth for several months. In the end, George simply removed the portrait and would accept not a penny, though the club offered to pay him half the amount stipulated in the original contract. It was the only completely humiliating incident of the artist's entire professional career.

In spite of this difficulty, which so depleted him emotionally, George found to his amazement, when he added up his earnings at the end of 1915, that his income had been sixty-five hundred dollars, a very important sum for that period, especially when we recall that most successful painters then derived a very substantial portion of their revenues from portraits, which was not the case with Bellows.

January of 1916 witnessed the arrival in New York of a figure who had rocked every person who had come into her life and who had even made the whole earth tremble just a little. This was the American dancer Isadora Duncan, one of the major eccentrics of our history. In the career of this extraordinarily magnetic woman it has been difficult for biographers to separate fact from fiction. Miss Duncan spared no effort to make the task harder by her insistence on living what amounted to a legend from the moment she first made her presence felt on this bemused planet. This initial impact upon the public consciousness occurred in New York just before the young George Bellows arrived from Columbus; her barefoot "imitations" of the dances she stoutly assured the press had been the style of ancient Greece were hooted off the stage and into the headlines. In the capitals of Europe, Isadora had fared somewhat better. She easily found rich and indulgent patrons who were willing to endow her lavish productions and even to father her children without troubling her with the encumbrances of wedlock—an institution she maintained, even in 1916, to be dedicated to the enslavement of the free spirit she certainly was.

Approaching forty, Isadora Duncan had returned to New York with a reputation so stained by tragedy (all three of her children were dead) that its comical and notorious aspects created about her an aura of larger-than-lifeness, a kind of mad magnificence. She inhabited a world of her mind's creation. The performances she offered this winter of 1916 were greeted with wild enthusiasm by audiences who lived in constant hope that she would do something to titillate their shabby little taste for scandal. But Isadora, who imagined that those who attended her productions did so to see her improvise, to see her create, thought herself idolized—and, in the main, this was enough for her; what she imagined to be true *was* true. Only rarely, as in Chicago later on, did she understand the prurience of her audiences; then, in a rage of frustration, she interrupted her dance, paused at center stage, and stripped herself to the waist. "There," she howled furiously. *"That's* what you wanted to see, isn't it?" And indeed it was. Policemen waiting in the wings happily bundled her off to jail.

Isadora Duncan was fearless, arrogant, and mysteriously endearing to men, who had not seen anyone to equal her in passion or straightforward speech. In a world where women were brought up to be submissive, she was aggressive. It is easy to understand that George Bellows was attracted to her. During her stay in New York, he and Emma were frequently her guests; and she returned the compliment by coming quite frequently to their house in Nineteenth Street.

What is more difficult to comprehend is George's attraction for Isadora. He was tall and good-looking, in a regular sort of way, if almost totally bald by now. But there was not a trace of mystery about him. Whatever else they are, athletes are rarely baffling personalities, even when they become artists. George Bellows was an instinctive artist; there was nothing of the intellectual about him. And as we shall note later on, when he allowed theory as such to intrude in a doctrinaire fashion upon his art, it was not beneficial. Perhaps, therefore, it was the spontaneity in his nature that appealed to Isadora, who was the most impulsive woman of her generation.

Whatever the explanation, Emma Bellows was well aware of the mutual attraction, and in a remarkable display of intelligent forbearance and feminine intuition, she bowed out of the scene to allow George and Isadora to discover whether or not their destinies were, as the dancer genuinely believed, inextricably intertwined. One evening, when the Bellowses were invited to Miss Duncan's apartment, Emma pleaded a diplomatic headache and urged her husband to go without her. She awaited his return with mingled amusement and curiosity, for she had told George flatly that Isadora would ask him to be the father of her next child. Bellows couldn't believe his ears—not so much, we must presume, for what Emma said, but for the fact that it was Emma saying it, and of *him*. Yet when he came home, very early, from his visit to Isadora, his expression was of astonishment and annoyance. "Did she ask you?" his wife inquired with a smile. George could only flush and nod. Nothing amazed him more than Emma's peal of delighted laughter. Clearly, he would never wholly understand women, and it didn't console him much that he had a lot of company.

What is interesting about this anecdote, aside from the insight it provides into the private life of Isadora Duncan (which, for the most part, she conducted in full public view, and meant to), is the light it throws on the character of George Bellows. He had been living in New York for almost twelve years now. Almost all his friends belonged to what was then called the "Washington Square Crowd" —later to be known as the "Greenwich Village Crowd." As a group, they were not very concerned with the proprieties that most Americans held dear—or said they did. "Bourgeois behavior" was a term of very great scorn around lower Fifth Avenue. Marital infidelity was not uncommon, and it was almost never condemned.

Though it affected much of the community to which the Bellowses and their closest friends belonged, this disrespect for the "respectable" seems not to have touched any of them—the Henris, the Speichers, the Sloans, and (when Kroll married) the Leon Krolls. It was equally typical of the Washington Square scene that marital fidelity was acceptable behavior, too. The objects of universal condemnation were priggishness, false modesty, prurience, prudery, and false pride. It still surprises some self-appointed moralists to find that these are sins condemned in Holy Writ.

Once Isadora Duncan had moved on to sensational successes elsewhere in the United States, the Bellows household settled back into familiar and pleasant routines. But there was innovation, too. For it was in this winter of 1916 that George began to make lithographs.

Lithography was hardly a new artistic medium. It had been invented by a German in the late eighteenth century. But master lithographers had been few in the intervening years. At the end of his long life, when his eyesight was failing, the great Spanish artist Francisco Goya, who had been making etchings since the beginning of his career in Madrid, turned to this new technique of drawing with wax crayon or pencil on a smooth, absorbent stone, because it was less demanding on his vision and lent itself readily to powerful, sweeping gestures and to dramatic shading. Honoré Daumier, the French painter and cartoonist of the middle of the nineteenth century, used lithography for his angrily satirical drawings, and lifted cartooning to the level of high art.

But no serious American artist had ever made serious, prolonged use of the lithographic technique until George Bellows turned to it in 1916. During the nine years of life that were left to him, he created nearly two hundred lithographs—a very considerable body of work, in which he revealed from the beginning a debt to both Goya and Daumier, in manner and politico-social outlook. The freedom of the technique allowed him to retain that element of spontaneity that was, as we have repeatedly observed, the hallmark of his best creations.

For the first of his lithographs, Bellows turned back to subjects that he had painted and sketched before—*Stag at Sharkey's*, *Prayer Meeting*, and *Hungry Dogs*. So delighted was he with the results, that he took as many as sixty proofs from each engraved stone before effacing the image so that the surface might be used again. *Collier's* commissioned him to make a series of three lithographs illustrating the boxing style of Jess Willard, "the great white hope," for which he received three hundred dollars. The best of the resulting prints is called, simply, *Training Quarters*.

In February, his old friend Emma Goldman was in trouble again, this time for making a speech in spirited defense of birth control. At the request of Anthony Comstock, a prominent New Yorker who had set himself up as semi-official guardian of the city's morals, the fiery anarchist was arrested. On the eve of her trial a couple of months later, all her supporters gathered for a party in the Hotel Brevoort on Fifth Avenue, just north of Washington Square, to gather funds for her defense. The Bellowses, the Sloans, and the Henris attended this gala to bear witness to Miss Goldman's inalienable right to express with absolute freedom her convictions on a subject that remains the topic of dispute more than a half century later. The magistrate who heard the case wasn't a bit impressed. Emma Goldman was found guilty of disturbing the peace and sentenced to serve fifteen days in jail or to pay a fine of one hundred dollars. Friends passed the hat again to collect enough for the latter penalty—though Miss Goldman herself believed that the right thing to do was to go to prison. She was ultimately convinced, however, that she could cause more embarrassment to civic officials if she were at liberty than if she were to spend a fortnight behind bars.

In early June, George and his family, including the Storys, left to spend the summer in Camden, Maine, where almost at once the painter found himself starved for male companionship. Leon Kroll agreed to join them. The shipyards of Camden attracted Bellows' attention very early during his stay there, and for nearly a month he made sketches and, later, paintings of the intense activity—

Teamster, Shipyard Society, Builders of Ships, and *Skeleton.*
(The skeleton in this case was the oaken framework of a
vessel.)

The tranquillity of Camden life was interrupted by the
first reports of the anarchist bombings that had attended
a Preparedness Day parade in San Francisco. A number of
people had been killed in these incidents. Violence in the
name of peace is not a new form of demonstration. The
purported leader of the San Francisco anarchist group was
Thomas J. Mooney, a long-time leader in the labor movement, like Big Bill Haywood. Mooney was tried for his
alleged role in these offenses and sentenced to death. From
this time until 1918, when the penalty was commuted to
life imprisonment, Tom Mooney's cause was a great concern of all radicals, socialist as well as anarchist, all of
whom firmly believed that there was a systematic and
semi-official effort being mounted from Washington to per-
suade the American people of the necessity of our intervention in the European war at the earliest possible moment. Bellows vigorously disapproved of the slaughter of
innocents in San Francisco, or anywhere else, but he disapproved, too, of capital punishment. This issue was, as
it remains, a terrible dilemma.

The Mooney case failed to distract the artist completely
from his work in Maine. His stay was brightened vastly by
word from a dealer in New York that a painting he had
based on sketches made during his frustrating summer in
Charlottesville, *In Virginia,* had just been sold for two
thousand dollars, a sum so great that he had at first dis-
believed the report. After Labor Day, George and Emma
sent their children back to the city with her parents and
saw Anna Bellows off to Columbus, leaving them alone for
the next two months—a real holiday. He continued to paint,
taking inspiration from a delightful return visit, with his

wife this time, to Matinicus Island and the nearby village of Criehaven—twin themes he would draw upon often in his later painting. And when they returned to their rented house in Camden, it was full autumn. George painted a series of canvases of the fall coloring in tones so vivid that Leon Kroll, when he saw them, considered them his friend's finest work.

While they were still cherishing the peace of Camden, George learned how futile it was to try to escape the sort of responsibility that was the penalty of fame. The directors of the Corcoran Art Gallery in Washington asked him to organize an exhibition of paintings by contemporary American artists. He willingly complied with this request because it would offer the national capital an opportunity to see for the first time not only his own work, but that of "The Eight," and of younger painters of promise—Henry McFee, Max Weber, Guy Pène duBois, Rockwell Kent, and Leon Kroll.

With the family reunited in New York, George turned in early November to a painting of his older daughter, Anne, holding a Japanese parasol, the first of a series of portraits of his children in which he recorded, with a charm inspired by love, their growth and glowing beauty. This picture soon found its way into the collection of Stephen C. Clark, the first Bellows he was to own, where it enjoyed an only temporary home—as we shall see.

The artist also resumed his lithography, picking up where he had left off on his departure for Maine. By the end of 1916 he noted in his catalog/journal that he had completed twenty-eight lithographs, taking from each stone an average of fifty proofs. In addition to prints devoted to boxing, he made several of members of his family, a landscape or two, and a number whose satirical commentary was sharp: *Benediction in Georgia, The Old Rascal* (reminiscent of Daumier), and *Reducing*—this last lithograph so caustic in its observation of the feminine passion for losing weight that it made the critic Royal Cortissoz fly into a rage against what he characterized as Bellows' love of ugliness.

This accusation, which would be made for more than a generation against all the painters of the so-called "Ashcan School," reminds some historians of art that precisely the same charge was leveled against Goya in his time. Indeed, there was a group of Spanish intellectuals, banded together from approximately 1785 to 1823, who called themselves the *acalofilos*, the lovers of ugliness. There is no evidence whatever to suggest that Sloan or Glackens or Bellows, the mainstays of early social realism in America, were consciously imitating this earlier association; they probably didn't even know of it. But they were certainly aware of the political and sociological implications of their art, and they made no pretense of lofty detachment from the world around them. Certain qualities in American society made them very angry, and their anger not only shows but was intended to show. To maintain, as some commentators have tried to do, that "social realism" was devoid of political motivation is absurd. We have only to look at the work itself to perceive this, and beyond the work are the men, quite as politically committed as artists of any land in any other age have ever been—and more so than some. (It is much less ridiculous to think Bellows' lithographs political than Picasso's doves, or even *Guernica*, that Spanish master's enigmatic hymn of sorrow to the horrors of the civil war in his native land.)

Anne Bellows was in her sixth year on this earth—a remarkably independent and ingenious little girl who had learned to arrange life for herself in a household that was really not organized to accommodate ordinary children.

One anecdote of this period illustrates her capacity to cope with her eccentric environment. As in most houses, children in the Bellows house were instructed to eat everything placed in front of them. Like many children, Anne had no great fondness for some of the dishes she was invited to consume. To avoid finishing the delicacies she didn't relish, she arranged at the little table where she ate by herself places for three guests who were invariably absent. She would allocate to each empty plate a portion of the unwanted food. When a visitor inquired one day who the missing parties were, Anne replied without hesitation, "God, Rembrandt, and Emma Goldman," three names often pronounced in that house.

January 1917 was a good month for George Bellows. Two of his paintings received awards, from the Pennsylvania Academy of Fine Arts and from the National Academy of Design. The former, *A Day in June,* was soon purchased for one thousand dollars. But January was a poor month for the United States, and the months that followed caused the artist and many other pacifists to re-examine their positions. For it was increasingly evident that the country would soon enter the European war—in spite of Woodrow Wilson's successful presidential campaign slogan: "He kept us out of war." The President waited for a little more than a month after his second inauguration, in March, before asking Congress for a formal declaration of war against the powers of the Triple Alliance.

Bellows was disturbed by conflicting emotions. As a devoted believer in a truly democratic society, he could appreciate the desperate straits in which Britain and France found themselves, especially in the spring of 1917, after the withdrawal of Russia from the war. Yet there was much about the foreign policies of those two powers that was dismaying to anyone who detested imperialism and colonialism. (Americans tended then, as now, not to consider their own country's behavior in Latin America in such terms.) So it was with greatest reluctance, for his pacifism and anti-colonialism were very strong feelings, that George announced himself in favor of Wilson's proposal.

The lithographs the artist made during that tumultuous period reveal his confusion. *Prepare, America,* for instance, is a bitter attack against the feverishness of the propagandists favoring our participation in the war. In *Electrocution,* doubtless inspired by the death penalty that still hung over the head of Tom Mooney, he showed that his preoccupation was not entirely about the European conflict. *Dance in a Madhouse* harks back to his visit, years before, to the mental hospital in Columbus. *Sawdust Trail* is a not very kind study of Billy Sunday at work. We find in a series called *Life Class,* reflecting his year of teaching in 1910–11 at the Art Students League, an effort to relieve himself of the cares of the world. But the most singular of all the lithographs he made in 1917 is *Christ Condemned,* the first religious picture he ever composed, which appeared in one of the final editions of *The Masses;* that radical monthly ceased publication before the year was out. One of the first victims of a war that has popular support is a press that is opposed to it.

George's former patron, Joseph Thomas of Lakewood, arranged for him to paint the portrait of Paul Clark, young son of a wealthy family living in San Mateo, California. The painter welcomed the opportunity to travel to the West Coast, which he had never visited. He went alone to Carmel, where he rented a house large enough for Emma and the children. In order to cover the great distances of the West, he bought a splendid big Buick phaeton and taught himself to drive it before his wife arrived.

The summer in the region of Carmel was probably the

most exciting of his life. Everything was new. The scenery of the Big Sur and Pebble Beach was magnificent—and empty, unlike the crowded beaches of the East. The Clarks were so pleased with the portrait of their son that they undertook to obtain other commissions from their opulent friends. (This success in portraiture was to prove unique in Bellows' career.)

The only blemish in their three-month stay in California was a severe attack of tonsillitis that placed George in the hospital for about ten days. Because of her Christian Science faith, Emma regarded her husband's complaint as self-indulgent and refused to visit him during his confinement.

He made a number of paintings while living at Carmel—notably *Sand Team* (depicting a gang of men attending the operation of a horse-drawn sand shovel—very much in the Bellows idiom) and *Golf Course,* a picture of the famous links at beautiful Pebble Beach. It was painful for both Emma and George to leave the West Coast. He sensed, perhaps, that he would never pass that way again, and wanted to extend his stay as long as possible—in spite of his commitment to teach once again at the Art Students League.

He arranged for a substitute at the League for the first two months, and at the beginning of October drove Emma and the children to Santa Fe, New Mexico, where they visited the Henris and the Krolls, who were spending a year in that old mission town. He also paid a call on Mabel Dodge at Taos, where the motor heiress had created a colony of artists and writers. The Taos life seemed to Bellows too much like a hothouse, totally disconnected from the realities of the world. He politely declined an invitation to spend a season there.

By the middle of November, the Bellowses were back in New York. They had made the long journey from New

Mexico by train, transporting the Buick east on a flatcar. George took up his post at the Art Students League and caught up on the news of his world—of art and of his friends. He was particularly impressed by a retrospective exhibition of the paintings of the Philadelphian Thomas Eakins, whom he described as "one of the best of all the world's masters." This judgment seems a little exaggerated unless we see it in the context of Eakins' death only the year before. Recent death does wonders for one's reputation.

Early in 1918, Bellows attended a series of lectures presented by Jay Hambidge, a Canadian-born painter and illustrator who had developed a theory to which he had given the galvanic title of "Dynamic Symmetry." George was immediately sympathetic to Hambidge's ideas; and with typical zeal, he adopted them as his own, at once seeking to apply them to his work.

Hambidge's concept was essentially geometric—that there are certain arrangements of rectangles and triangles that, given the dimensions of a canvas and the relative proportions of the objects to be depicted, happily or adversely affect the aesthetic properties of a painting. Just why this approach to art (which had evolved from architectural studies of Gothic styles stimulated in the nineteenth century by the popular revival of that mode of construction) should so have stirred George Bellows, we cannot explain with certainty. He was not an intellectual painter and, as we have seen, he greatly resented the stern dictates of the academicians.

Perhaps, in the light of what George had seen of cubism five years before at the Armory Show, Hambidge's strictures about the "emotional geometry" of a picture struck a responsive chord. By learning something more about the relationships between planes in cubist canvases, Bellows began to comprehend this aspect of "modernism." It is certainly too much to suggest that George had any intention of becoming a cubist. What he did do was to adopt Hambidge's doctrines of rectangulation and triangulation in many of the pictures he composed after he had fully absorbed that older man's philosophy. Max Weber, an artist whom Bellows had helped and admired, also became an apostle of Hambidge—but unlike George, the younger Weber managed to create on the basis of the Canadian's mathematical formulas paintings that were entirely original. For Bellows, Dynamic Symmetry seemed rather to impose itself on him superfluously, like an unneeded outer garment.

George was not so full of Hambidge that he was unable to function as an artist. Indeed, he had undergone a further political transformation in the months since his return from the West. The trumpets of war propaganda had reached his ears, and he was heeding them. No longer were his feelings about American involvement tepid. Tales of German atrocities (which many had originally dismissed and some were still dismissing) inspired a series of sixteen lithographs on war themes that he accomplished in April and May. Some of the titles suggest the matter: *The Enemy Arrive, Massacred, The Last Victim, Sergeant Delaney*.

Of all these lithographs, the one in which Bellows illustrated the execution of Nurse Edith Cavell by the Germans in 1915 was the most popular with collectors. The tale itself was and remains a most poignant and tragic episode of the war; the British nurse was put to death for aiding wounded Allied soldiers who wished to escape from the prison hospital of which she was in charge. An exhibition of the whole series of Bellows' war lithographs was held in Keppel's Gallery in New York, where they enjoyed an unprecedented success—though William Allison (who was assistant manager of the gallery and later became the artist's principal dealer) found many of them almost unbearably powerful, comparable, he said, only with Goya's most fearful collection of etchings, *The Disasters of War*.

With the Speichers, the Bellowses decided to spend the summer of 1918 somewhat nearer New York than Maine, choosing Middletown, Rhode Island—not far from Newport. One reason for wanting to be comparatively near the city was that both George and Eugene Speicher had put down their names as volunteers for the newly organized Tank Corps—second only to the Air Corps in glamour. They expected to be called to service before the summer was out. This was not to occur. In fact, they weren't called to the colors at all.

Bellows' obsession with the war continued throughout the summer vacation in Rhode Island. He reversed his customary procedure by making paintings based on his earlier lithographs—*The Enemy Arrive, Massacre at Dinant, The Barricade*, and (inevitably) *The Execution of Edith Cavell*. He sent the first of these paintings to Keppel's as soon as it was dry. With considerable personal distaste, but with a clear understanding of the excitement it would generate, William Allison immediately placed it in the window of the gallery. Charles Dana Gibson, dean of American illustrators, proclaimed *The Enemy Arrive* to be the finest thing he had ever seen. Frank Crowninshield, editor of *Vanity Fair*, stated in print that it was the best thing to be seen on Fifth Avenue—which seems something of a left-handed compliment, but it was apparently not so intended. Crowninshield truly admired Bellows.

When George's painting of Edith Cavell's execution was displayed in the same setting the following September, it received from nearly everyone a quantity of praise that had a great deal more to do with the emotional impact of the subject matter than the quality of the picture itself. The painter's rendering of the scene was highly dramatic; he made use of intense light and shadow to enhance the pathos of the incident. Only a single voice was raised against the painting, that of Joseph Pennell, an etcher of distinction who could (and frequently did) call himself that rarest of things, a friend of the great James Whistler (who had prided himself on his mastery of "the gentle art of making enemies"). Pennell strongly criticized Bellows for daring to depict an incident of which he had no firsthand knowledge. Few artists have ever been handed such a perfect straight line, and we must always be grateful to Bellows for not muffing this golden chance to give the classic reply: "I haven't ever heard that Leonardo had a ticket of admission to the Last Supper."

On Armistice Day, November 11, 1918, George Bellows was completing another war painting, *The Return of the Useless*, in which he showed a group of northern French peasants being passed through allied lines after their German captors had rejected them as no longer fit to work in the fields to gather in the enemy's harvest. Hardly had the great news been announced to the rejoicing world than the artist received a communication from Sir Joseph Duveen, the most illustrious dealer in Renaissance art of his day. Duveen was representing Miss Helen Clay Frick, sister of the steel magnate and partner of J. P. Morgan. Miss Frick, the dealer informed the artist, would pay five hundred dollars each for a pair of large mural-type panels celebrating the termination of the war that, President Wilson had assured his millions of constituents, would make the world safe for democracy. The two paintings, ten feet in height, were the worst pictures George Bellows ever composed. In this respect, however, he could take a little heart from the axiom whose proof is everywhere to behold, that public art is almost always ghastly. His was no worse than most, nor much better, either.

The Final Years

Many historians believe that the year 1919 was the most fateful in the entire history of the Western world. The major powers that had participated on the victorious side in the war attempted to impose on the losers, Germany and the Austro-Hungarian Empire (which by then was in ruins), a treaty of peace whose terms, especially as they applied to reparations for economic loss and property damage, were impossibly severe. The Germans, upon whom the main burden fell, were both unwilling and unable to pay, a condition that helped mightily in the creation of the Nazi state and the destruction of the Third Republic of France.

More disastrous still, in the opinion of detached observers, was the failure of the United States Senate to ratify President Wilson's proposal that this country join the League of Nations, an organization that was conceived to be a crucial support of the very shaky structure of peace that had been put together at Versailles. But the mood of the majority of Americans was to be demonstrated clearly in the presidential election of 1920, when Warren G. Harding was named to the office on the strength of a campaign promising a "return to normalcy," by which was meant to return to conditions as they had been before the war—to what would later be termed "isolationism."

The issues that really made America tremble in 1919 had nothing to do with the war or the peace—two amendments to our Constitution, which had been duly passed by both houses of the Congress and were now being circulated among the legislatures of the several states for approval. One would give women the right to vote. The other would prohibit the transportation, manufacture, and sale of beverages containing more than 3.2 per cent of alcohol by volume.

There was a surprising amount of controversy over the question of woman suffrage. The most sensational speculations were offered, by men, in opposition to this amendment —their essence being that women were more frivolous than men and would, therefore, cast their votes unreasonably. The validity of that particular line of argument could best be measured by ratification of the Eighteenth Amendment, the Prohibition amendment, which was the accomplishment of men—a measure not merely frivolous but downright insane. After its passage into law, the amendment was not enforced on any major scale, because it was unenforceable. By the time of its repeal in 1933, it had resulted in the creation of an empire of crime and a nation of lawbreakers; to take an illegal drink had become symbolic of "striking a blow for liberty."

George Bellows supported the Nineteenth Amendment, which became law in 1921. And though he was not a drinker himself he strongly opposed the Eighteenth (which took effect in 1919) as an invasion of privacy. As usual, however, he didn't allow his political convictions to keep him from his work—nor, in this instance, did he allow them expression in drawings or lithographs.

By the war's end, he was on the brink of a spectacular increase in popularity and sales. The prospect of a one-man exhibition in the most reputable gallery in New York,

Knoedler's, spurred him during the first months of 1919 to prodigious labors. Of the paintings he made before the show's opening in April, three deserve mention: *Old Lady with a Blue Book, Anne in Blue-Green Silk,* and *The Studio*—the last an entertaining conversation piece devoted to the balconied attic of the house in Nineteenth Street, in which he represented himself at work and all the members of his household and a number of friends engaged in a variety of activities.

The show at Knoedler's was a success beyond George Bellows' most fantastic dreams of avarice. Four of his small oils painted at Monhegan brought five hundred dollars each; *Golf Course* (Pebble Beach), *The Circus* (dating to the summer of 1912), and *Polo Crowd* (from 1910) brought two thousand dollars, twenty-five hundred dollars, and three thousand dollars respectively. After making deductions for the gallery's commission, he made from that single exhibition as much as he had earned in his most prosperous previous year.

While his paintings were still on display at Knoedler's, Mrs. Chester Dale, wife of one of the country's most discriminating collectors of art, asked him to paint her portrait. And once again, as had so often happened in the past, George Bellows found the task difficult, for he didn't much like the arrogant, demanding Maud Dale. During the months of April, May, and June, he slaved over several versions of the portrait, none of them successful. The artist insisted that the main problem was caused by his sitter's demand that her little dog be featured in the picture. Another was that Mrs. Dale made George come to her home, so he was compelled to work in unfamiliar surroundings, and always at hours convenient to her rather than to him. Finally, with outspoken reluctance, Maud Dale accepted a portrait. In addition to expressing her displeasure with the picture, she gave it as her opinion that the painter was "a bit vulgar, a bit too loud."

The Bellowses went once more to Middletown for the summer, where, as if to prove to himself that he *could* paint fine portraits, he made two of his beloved Emma, one in a purple dress, another in a black print. Of the former he wrote, "I think I have painted my best portrait of Emma and a rare picture. A hand and an eye, the width of the shadow side of the head are still in question."

As it happened, the Chester Dales were vacationing at nearby Newport, and George was prevailed on to have another bash at portraying the formidable Maud. He made two supplementary pictures of her that season, for which her husband paid three thousand dollars, but the artist liked neither of them (sharing the view of the subject), and he accepted the sum because he had given the best part of three months to the various efforts.

A charming painting accomplished at Middletown that summer is *On the Porch*, in which Bellows portrayed his daughters with their cousin, Margaret Story. After the exertions of the spring with its exasperating portrait sessions, he was content to take his ease, to play tennis, swim, play a little baseball, and do a few sketches. He meant to enjoy the luxury of a holiday over which, for the first time in living memory, hung no shadows of financial or personal disaster.

Not even the news that his dear old friend Joe Taylor and his family were coming to New York for a few weeks could lure George back to the city—though he lent the professor his house, and wrote him lengthy instructions about what he should try to see during his visit, whom he should try to meet. One of the metropolitan sights he advised Taylor not to miss was Petitpas, a restaurant and rooming house run by three Frenchwomen, which was a haunt of artists and writers. George wrote that his friend would most surely find at Petitpas the Irish painter John Butler Yeats, father of the celebrated poet and of the impressionistic painter Jack Yeats. The garrulous old man lived at Petitpas (supported mainly by the generosity of the Irish-American John Quinn), where he made much and often amusing and occasionally brilliant conversation.

But in August, George felt that he had to return briefly to New York, to help in the selection of paintings and sculpture for an exhibition of contemporary American art that was to be hung in the splendid Luxembourg Palace in Paris. A similar show of French work was to be presented in New York. George's eagerness had nothing to do with his own pictures being represented; by 1919, that was a matter of course. His concern, rather, was for younger painters, especially for Max Weber, who, as we have observed, shared Bellows' enthusiasm for the theories of Jay Hambidge.

When he returned to Middletown toward the end of the month, he was filled once more with eagerness and energy for painting, and produced a number of interesting canvases, some devoted to rustic scenes he had not hitherto treated—*Young Horse Grazing, Five Cows, Bull and Horses, Black Bull, A Boy and a Calf*. Other pictures were new encounters with familiar themes—*Red Sun, Fog Curtain, Dark Day*, and two pictures called *Tennis at Newport*. He completed the summer holiday with the entire family by making two fine portraits of Anna Bellows, whom he called "the biggest mother in captivity"—*Grandma Bellows* and *Old Lady with a Bonnet*.

George and Emma remained in Middletown for about a month after seeing the others of the household off to New York and Columbus. It was their quiet time, and they were to require the sustenance it gave them, for the au-

tumn and winter to come were rigorous. A joint exhibition
of the work of Bellows and John C. Johannesen opened
at the Albright Gallery in Buffalo in October and was then
transferred to the Art Institute of Chicago. To coincide
with the November opening in the nation's second city,
George was invited to lecture for two months at the Institute for a stipend of one thousand dollars per month,
twice what he had been paid by the Art Students League
for a full academic year less than a decade before. He accepted the offer with enthusiasm because he enjoyed
teaching and, perhaps even more, because he could spread
the message of Jay Hambidge's Dynamic Symmetry.

Leaving their daughters in the care of the Storys, the
Bellowses traveled to Chicago in early November and
found their stamina repeatedly tested by a round of din-
ners and receptions that continued through the two months
of their stay. Of the many important connections the artist
made in Chicago, none compared in purely personal appeal
with his introduction to Mrs. Mary Brown Tyler, an elderly
lady of very distinguished appearance whose portrait
George painted twice that autumn. He liked her hugely
and did her full justice on both occasions, yielding to
her request for anonymity by entitling the paintings *Mrs.
T.*—though immediately after he and Emma left Chicago,
Mrs. Tyler boasted to everyone she met of the portraits
that the celebrated George Bellows had insisted on making
of her.

The couple paused in Columbus on their way back to
New York, and remained there on learning that George's
half sister Laura Monett was in poor health. While still
in Ohio, a letter came from Eugene Speicher saying that
of the paintings Bellows had helped to select for the exhibition in the Luxembourg Palace in Paris, the "moderns"
had been excluded. A second communication from an

outraged Robert Henri confirmed this information, adding
the list of artists whose work had been displayed: Louis
Bouché, Bernard Gussow, Henry McFee, Alfred Henry
Maurer, Charles Sheeler, Joseph Stella, Max Weber, and
William Zorach.

What was in some doubt until Bellows returned to New
York was where the responsibility for these extraordinary
omissions lay. At a closed-door meeting of members of the
National Academy of Design who had selected the work
for the Paris exhibition, the matter was discussed at furious
length. Although no official statement was issued at the
conclusion of this session, a letter by Bellows that soon
afterward appeared in *The Arts* left little doubt. It was
not, as some in ignorance had suggested, the French
hosts, but the Americans who had supervised the mount-
ing of the show, who had been responsible for the pro-
hibitions. Bellows was offended by the entire fiasco, but
he was particularly mortified that the paintings of Max
Weber should have been banned, for this reflected on him
as a well-known advocate of Weber's pictures.

Outrage followed outrage. In the first week of January
1920, an exhibition at Knoedler's gave prominence to several of Bellows' recent paintings. Writing about this show
in the New York *Sun,* the critic Henry McBride singled
out George's contributions for a particularly strong and
bewildering attack: "'The Red Sun' is apparently painted
in aniline dyes, and 'The After Glow' also has a scheme
in yellow which can scarcely endure. Perhaps the artist
deliberately used dangerous colors in order to see what
would happen in a month or two."

To a long-time disciple of Hardesty Maratta who had
been passionately concerned about the quality and dura-
bility of his materials, this remarkable assault, coming right
on the heels of his disillusionment over the Luxembourg

show, provoked from Bellows an immediate and bitter reply: "Mr. McBride has endeavored, by the use of the words 'apparently,' 'scarcely,' and 'perhaps' to avoid a direct false and libellous charge . . . ; but I submit that his intent is plain and that he intended to charge me with dishonest practice in my profession as an artist, wherein the permanence of the material used is a fundamental thing, and of offering for sale paintings painted in fugitive colors. . . . I have always sought to use only colors of the highest standard of permanence. I have always held it as a high ideal that working for permanency was to the joy of the workman."

The *Sun* of January thirteenth printed George's letter in full, and immediately below it appeared Henry McBride's abject apology. Nearly forty years later, McBride was to write the introduction to the catalog of a large retrospective exhibition of Bellows' work in the National Gallery of Art in Washington. It is scarcely surprising that he made no allusion to the unfortunate episode.

A year or so earlier, Bellows had been introduced to Stephen Clark, one of the most discerning of American collectors—probably through Eugene Speicher's wife, Elsie, who had done interior decoration for members of the Clark family both in the city and in their country demesne of Cooperstown, New York. Clark had begun buying Bellows' pictures, already owning *The Skeleton* and *Anne with a Parasol*, both painted in 1916. In the last days of January, Clark expressed great admiration for a portrait of George's niece, Margaret Story, and said he would like to exchange the picture of Anne he now owned for that of Margaret. The artist declined on principle. Any picture of his that was offered for sale was worth owning, he said politely but firmly; he would not barter—and he didn't. Stephen Clark paid him fifteen hundred dollars for *Mar-*

garet, but made to himself the promise that one day he would make his trade with Bellows.

In February, George painted one of his finest portraits, of Waldo Peirce, the painter—demonstrating again his talent for giving warmth to pictures of those he liked. Peirce was certainly likable, and colorful. Two years Bellows' junior, Peirce was a native of Bangor, Maine, a classmate and intimate of John Reed at Harvard. His most extravagant exploit had been at Reed's expense in 1911, when the two set out for Europe on a freighter; just after the ship cleared Boston harbor, Peirce changed his mind, leaped over the side, and swam to shore. On reaching Europe, Reed was arrested and briefly held on the charge of murdering his friend. During the war, Peirce had driven an ambulance, been wounded, decorated, and discharged. With his friend Ernest Hemingway, whose portrait is one of Peirce's finest works, he wandered for a time in Spain before returning to America. Bellows' portrait of Peirce was dispatched almost at once to the Corcoran Gallery in Washington for an exhibition of contemporary art. The painter was annoyed to note in the catalog of this show that the portrait was listed as Waldo Peirce's property and therefore not for sale. A corrective letter to the editor served no purpose but to assuage the anger of its writer.

This was just another of a number of minor irritations that marked the winter of 1920. None was of real importance; yet, taken collectively, they made George restless and unproductive. So when Eugene Speicher invited him and Emma to visit them at Woodstock, New York, where he and Elsie had recently bought a house, Bellows seized the chance joyfully, left the two children with the Storys, and bundled Emma off to the Catskills. Though they stayed at Woodstock for nearly two months, George accomplished practically nothing in the way of work. But the tranquillity of the setting, the brooding omnipresence of the impressive mountains that flanked every road, appealed to him so much that he rented Shotwell House, near the Speichers', for the following summer.

When they returned briefly to New York in late May, both George and Emma separately wrote his Aunt Fanny, now widowed in San Diego, inviting her to join her sister Anna and the rest of the family for the summer at Woodstock. In his letter, the painter added that he and his mother planned to make the rest of her life more comfortable by providing her with an annual income of one thousand dollars from each of them; for Sam Daggett had not been able to leave her much of an estate. The old lady accepted both offers and invitation with glowing gratitude. This and other examples of George Bellows' compassionate concern, not only for his own relations, but for Emma's, too, are among his many attractive qualities. He performed similar acts of generosity for friends, especially younger artists. There are probably other painters who have been as temperate and gentle as Bellows, but the single example of Peter Paul Rubens again leaps to mind as one who was comparably kind, sensible, and sensitive.

Shotwell House in Woodstock that summer of 1920 was very much a family scene—and George made use of his relatives in the paintings he made in those months. He portrayed his Aunt Fanny as *The Old Lady in Black,* and in a picture he composed with Jay Hambidge's doctrine very much in his mind, he painted his aunt, his mother, and his younger daughter, *Elinor, Jean and Anna,* one of the most tender of his portraits. "Elinor" properly spelled would have been "Eleanor"—his Aunt Fanny. After Labor Day, George and Emma stayed on at Shotwell House to enjoy the peace and the brilliant autumn coloring of the Catskills.

Ever since the meeting the previous January of the National Academy of Design to discuss the humiliation of younger and/or more *avant-garde* artists at the Luxembourg Palace, George Bellows and others had been planning to organize another federation that would give such creative spirits fairer representation. The foundation of the New Society of American Artists was marked by an article from Bellows' pen that appeared in a fall issue of *Vanity Fair*, the magazine that Frank Crowninshield's editorial genius had made the country's most fashionable. The article coincided with the Society's first exhibition, which, as Bellows wrote, would emphasize the work of younger artists who didn't wish to conform to the styles found acceptable by the Academy. He himself showed here for the first time *Elinor, Jean and Anna*. This painting and the show in general were well received and widely covered by the press —for by late 1920, the judgment of the public had been altered not only by the Armory Show but by several postwar exhibitions of advanced European art.

Later that year, *Elinor, Jean and Anna* was awarded the Beck Medal by the Pennsylvania Academy of Fine Arts, though press reaction to the picture in Philadelphia was not at all enthusiastic. *Old Lady in Black*, hung in an exhibition of the National Arts Club in New York, was accorded the first prize of six hundred dollars and sold to a collector from Des Moines, Iowa, for three thousand dollars —the second time a Bellows had attained such a price. So impressed were the club's directors by Bellows' performance and success that they asked him to give a talk at their annual meeting. Characteristically, he elected not to speak about himself, but about American painting of the twentieth century—singling out as the masters of the previous generation Winslow Homer, Thomas Eakins, and Albert Ryder; Ryder's death three years before had passed almost unnoticed, and it would be a long time before his reputation lived up to George's estimate of it. Of living artists, he praised his friend John Sloan, whom he called "the greatest living etcher and a very great artist." Whether or not Sloan deserved such lavish praise, he certainly needed it financially.

A meeting just before Christmas drew George Bellows back to lithography, which he had virtually abandoned for two years and more. He had never made his own prints, leaving this to the skill of trained hands. His introduction to Bolton Brown, painter of landscapes, lecturer and writer on art subjects, and master engraver, provided the impetus for a return to lithography. Brown, who was seventeen years older than Bellows, was probably the most competent figure in his field, in terms of pure printing technique. He readily agreed to work with George, whose early lithographs he had much admired. All the equipment for making prints was installed on the balcony floor of the studio in Nineteenth Street. There, for the next four years, Bolton Brown was a permanent fixture.

During the first three months of 1921, the two men produced the astounding number of sixty finished lithographs, an average of approximately one for every working day. The subjects were wildly various—most of them taken from themes that Bellows had already sketched or painted: nudes, sporting scenes, family portraits, and anecdotal material. Most interesting of this prolific output were *Holdup,* *Snowstorm,* and a nostalgic evocation of Bellows' youth in Ohio, *Sunday Morning, 1897, Going to Church,* very much the kind of illustration that Norman Rockwell would later make his trademark. George was so pleased with the skill of his new partner that he insisted that Bolton Brown add his signature to each of the fifty copies they made of every lithograph in the next four years.

Nostalgia appeared as well in two portraits of his mother that Bellows painted in March—both placing her in the sitting room of the Columbus house in which the artist had grown up. Anna Bellows, as her son portrayed her, was not a fraction less "the biggest mother in captivity" than she had been two years before, when he had good-naturedly so described her.

He was occupied also that spring with writing, completing an article for the June issue of *The American Art Student* devoted to the virtues of Jay Hambidge's theories. The following sentence from that piece summarizes the painter's evaluation of Hambidge's contribution to art: "The study of dynamic symmetry is probably more valuable than the study of anatomy." In a conversation, such a remark would be pardonable; in print, it is simply ridiculous. But it does suggest that had George encountered Hambidge earlier on in his career, he might have become a far more radical artist than the time allowed him at this stage in his short life. For out of purely theoretical and intellectual conceptions about art, like that of Dynamic Symmetry, emerged a philosophy that underlies abstract expressionism as we behold it in the work of Mondrian, Albers, and the entire geometry-mad school of Op Art.

All the Bellowses and Storys and Aunt Fanny Daggett gathered together once more in Shotwell House at Woodstock for the summer. But, for George, the season was twice interrupted—first to make the brief journey to Tuxedo Park to paint the portrait of Master Meredith Hare, whose mother, Mrs. Montgomery Hare, informed the artist that she had very definite ideas for the picture. Bellows again encountered problems in portraiture. He found the boy distinctly unlikable and the mother even more so —as he wrote Emma. Mrs. Hare was unable to decide between two poses that George had drawn. Thinking to improve matters, he made a third drawing, which served only to add to the mother's confusion. In the end, no portrait of Meredith Hare was ever painted. For the three sketches, however, Bellows accepted without a qualm a payment of fifteen hundred dollars and gratefully returned to Woodstock.

In July, he received an invitation from Herbert Bayard Swope, the magnetic editor of the New York *World,* to go to Jersey City to record for his newspaper the bout, promoted by Tex Rickard, between the popular French world light-heavyweight champion, Georges Carpentier, and Jack Dempsey, the world heavyweight champion, scheduled to take place on something called "Boyle's Thirty Acres." Both the remuneration and the subject were tempting. George agreed at once.

The fight, however, was a great disappointment. Dempsey knocked out Carpentier in the fourth round. In the circumstances, it would seem strange that an American crowd's sympathies should be on the side of the foreigner, but this was the case. Dempsey's victory was roundly denounced by the spectators, mainly because the American Legion had accused the challenger of being a draft dodger, an offense of a lot more gravity in 1921 than it is a half century later.

Though Bellows made a number of sketches of the bout, only one showed the favored Georges Carpentier in a happy light—the moment when he was introduced to the crowd before the fight began. Of this instant he made a formal drawing for the *World,* though in subsequent lithographs of that event in the hot July afternoon, he depicted the more active moments of Carpentier's brief encounter with the "Manassa Mauler."

Of the paintings Bellows made during the remainder of that summer, his portrait of the beautiful, young Katherine

Rosen, daughter of an artist-neighbor of Woodstock, is by a wide margin the best. When Stephen Clark saw it the next autumn in New York, he determined to possess it and, as we shall see, he had his way and on more or less his own terms.

Old Lady in Black, Bellows' portrait of his Aunt Fanny made in the summer of 1920, was awarded the Harris first prize of five hundred dollars by the Art Institute of Chicago in 1921, an event that may have induced Chester Dale to commission George to paint his portrait, which was completed in January 1922. With the bitterest recollections of his difficulties in painting Dale's wife a few years before, George applied himself with much diligence to this work—but as was too often so, diligence alone was not enough. There was little *rapport* between artist and subject, a condition the portrait immediately discloses; it is wooden and without much feeling. Dale accepted it and paid the stipulated fifteen-hundred-dollar fee, but he never bought another Bellows painting during the artist's lifetime.

Fortunately, there was no dearth of prizes or commissions that year. *Elinor, Jean and Anna* won a fifteen-hundred-dollar award from the Carnegie Institute of Pittsburgh as the best painting of its current exhibition that winter. And the success of George's illustrations for the *World* in July prompted the editors of *The Century Magazine* to request a large series of drawings to accompany the text of *The Wind Bloweth,* a novel by the popular Irish writer Donn Byrne, for which the artist received one hundred dollars each. Though he had no personal knowledge of Irish life and landscape, the descriptions provided in the book itself, supplemented by observations on the land of saints and scholars by old John Butler Yeats at Petitpas, and Henri's sketches from his summer in Ireland just before the war, provided Bellows with material so adequate that, in the opinion of some of his critics, these works were among his finest drawings.

In April, *Stag at Sharkey's*, which had so often been exhibited throughout the country but never sold, was finally purchased by the Cleveland Gallery of Art for fifteen hundred dollars—a real bargain. The title of the painting was, curiously, changed to *Club Night*, which has led to confusion in later years, for the picture that originally bore that name inherited the earlier title, *Stag at Sharkey's*. To clarify this matter, the painting in Cleveland is the second of the three pictures that George made of pugilistic evenings in Sharkey's Saloon. So it is not the canvas that shocked the lady guests who saw it during its brief exhibition in the Cleveland Athletic Club.

With this purchase fee and the proceeds from the drawings for *The Century*, George bought a piece of land at Woodstock and spent the late spring months planning the construction of a summer house there, and the first two months of summer in the actual building of it. Utilizing the knowledge of the building trades he had acquired as a youth in Columbus, and naturally trying his best to apply to the scheme the principles of Dynamic Symmetry in three dimensions, he and a constantly changing group of friends, mainly other artists who were summering in the region of the Catskills, constructed a house whose outlines were eccentric and whose austerity was positively puritanical. It had neither electricity nor inside plumbing. For the water supply, the artist devised a pump resembling the propulsion mechanism of a railroad handcar; this fed a supply tank. Since there was no refrigeration, items such as milk and butter were kept cool in a nearby brook.

The quarters were cramped for everyone but George, whose studio was commodious. It was the first and only house ever designed by George Bellows. By August, when the family moved from the comparative luxury of Shotwell House to the new building, the painter was so exhausted that he had no energy left during the balance of the summer for any other sort of work. But when the older and younger generations departed, leaving him and Emma alone, he did find the strength for painting again; the only picture of moment accomplished that fall, however, *The White Horse*, is a Catskill landscape much admired by Bellows enthusiasts for its romantic qualities that remind us a bit of the world of Charles Burchfield and Albert Ryder.

The success of his illustrations of the Donn Byrne novel for *The Century* was instrumental in his receiving a commission of greater importance from a more widely circulated Hearst publication, *The International Magazine*, to make a series of drawings based on H. G. Wells' most recent novel, *Men Like Gods*, for which the editors promised to pay thirty-eight hundred dollars, the largest sum yet offered for a Bellows commission. By Christmas of 1922, all the subjects had been selected and were at least in the form of rough sketches.

Shortly after the holiday, Stephen Clark once again broached to Bellows the subject of making an exchange —the portrait of Anne with a parasol for that of Katherine Rosen. And once again, the artist stood his original ground —for a time. He was not, he assured the eminent collector, in the business of swapping pictures (except with fellow artists). Under gentle but incessant pressure, he finally agreed to take back the portrait of his daughter in exchange for *Katherine Rosen* and thirteen hundred dollars. Looking back on it from the vantage point of half a century, the transaction seems to favor Stephen Clark—but Bellows was well pleased to have back in his possession *Anne with a Parasol*. After his death, Emma presented the portrait to her older daughter; it is one of the few family portraits that remained in Bellows hands.

Early in 1923 the artist began to make drawings far more systematically than had ever been his habit in the past. The impulse seems to have been occasioned by a commission from *The Century* for an illustration of an article about lynching—a subject too often in the news during the years following the return of black American soldiers from a Europe where they had enjoyed a freedom and welcome much more hospitable than anything they found in the South. The final drawing that Bellows produced for *The Century* he entitled *The Law Is Too Slow*, a little work that owes much of its savagery (as well as the bitter tone of its title) to Goya.

The report of a disaster in a coal mine, where working conditions were unspeakable in their inhumanity, prompted another drawing, *Dead Line*, a picture of relatives of the victims waiting for news at the pit head. He returned as well to subjects he had attacked before—Billy Sunday, in particular, who appeared in two drawings of this first half of 1923.

He didn't, however, confine himself to themes that suggested his anger. He drew portraits of members of his household and of friends, particularly the artist John Carroll, who lived near the Bellowses at Woodstock. Just before departing for the Catskills in June, George made a painting, *Introducing John L. Sullivan*, an amiable caricature of the current boxing scene. Sullivan, former world heavyweight champion, garishly dressed and extremely portly, had made an appearance in the ring at Boyle's Thirty Acres just before the start of the Dempsey-Carpentier fight. In George's picture he looked the very model of the successful ward politician, not the formidable reliquary that contained the ashes of one of the greatest fighters of all time. The painting evokes at the same time feelings of revulsion and sadness—and we must imagine that Bellows, though long a student of what A. J. Liebling (one of the few fine writers to deal with boxing) called "the sweet science," had these mixed emotions himself.

In July, installed in the house he had built the previous summer, Bellows followed up his earlier drawing of his neighbor John Carroll with a fine, sympathetic portrait of that artist. This work was just completed when he learned from Howard Monett, his nephew, that Anna Bellows, who had been too ill and too old to make the journey to Woodstock this year, was dying. In August, George and Emma made the sorrowful journey to Columbus to await her end. It was not slow in coming, and though it was infinitely painful for the painter to watch his mother softly waste away, there was some solace in the knowledge that she had lived a rich life after her own fashion, loving and being loved, and that her death was peaceful and without great agony.

When the Bellowses at last returned to Woodstock, the news that awaited them certainly helped to brighten the mood they had brought back with them from Columbus. The portrait of *Emma in a Black Print* had been purchased by a private Boston collector for three thousand dollars, and the Albright Gallery of Buffalo, which had given him an important exhibition a few years before, had bought *Elinor, Jean and Anna* from Knoedler's for a figure so unprecedentedly lofty that even after the gallery's commission had been deducted, the painter realized the princely sum of sixty-five hundred dollars. He had no trouble remembering the "good year" when he had grossed an identical amount for a full twelve months of strenuous work.

By way of celebration, he immediately began to paint

the portrait *Emma and Her Children,* a task that was interrupted by an assignment from the New York *Evening Journal* to cover the heavyweight championship fight between Jack Dempsey and the new challenger, Luis Firpo, at the Polo Grounds in New York. The bout was over in embarrassingly short order. Firpo was strong but extremely awkward. In the first round, he accidentally caught the champion with a blow that literally knocked him out of the ring—leading "good Americans" who were still suspicious of Dempsey's patriotism to hope that he would soon be the former champion. Their elation was premature. The "Manassa Mauler" flattened Firpo definitively in the second round. The most spectacular moment of the bout, however, had been Dempsey's unexpected flight into the arms of the first-row spectators; it was this instant that Bellows chose for his illustration for the *Journal*—a subject he would later lithograph and, ultimately, make the topic of his final painting of the ring.

After the Bellows children had returned to the city with their Story grandparents, George made a painting of *The Crucifixion,* basing this picture on an illustration he had made the year before for *The International Magazine* to accompany a story by Sir Arthur Conan Doyle. The painting, unique in the entire inventory of Bellows' work, was founded firmly in Jay Hambidge's precepts of Dynamic Symmetry. Most critics agree that it is not a great success, and though a considerable proportion of the paintings that were left to his widow have been sold, this one remains in the Bellows estate today. Nevertheless, when it was exhibited at the second show of the New Society of American Artists, it caused a sensation—perhaps in some measure because such a painting from the hand of George Bellows was in itself newsworthy. Its success was brief and entirely occasioned by the public. As we have already observed, it was never to be sold, and the press was as hostile to the work as it dared to be when commenting on an artist who was so well established a master. For at the beginning of the last year of his life, Bellows was probably the best-known serious artist of the day—a statement it would be difficult to establish as fact, for these matters were not any more measurable in 1924 than they are today.

A second Bellows painting of the summer of 1923, *Fisherman's Family,* a recollection of Monhegan Island almost a decade earlier, won a first prize at an exhibition in the Corcoran Art Gallery in Washington. And *My Mother,* of 1922, received the Logan purchase prize of the Chicago Art Institute in this same season. The Institute added seventeen hundred dollars to the award of five hundred dollars to acquire the painting for its collection.

In this period of his apogee as a public art figure, George accepted an invitation to lecture once again to the pupils of the Art Students League, and agreed as well to talk to those of the Masters' School. To every group, he preached the gospel according to Jay Hambidge. This new celebrity had no effect on him. He and Emma continued to live precisely as they had since their marriage, and there appears no reason to suppose that had Bellows been spared (or, as we shall see, had he seen fit to spare himself), they would have significantly altered their style of living. It satisfied them perfectly.

During the first three months of 1924, George and Bolton Brown turned out thirty-three lithographs, eight of them of nudes, others derived from the artist's illustrations of *The Wind Bloweth* and *Men Like Gods.* He made one satirical print that alluded to the coming presidential election campaign, *Appeal to the People,* and a single work devoted to the Dempsey-Firpo fight. One significant measure of the popularity George Bellows was now enjoying may be found in the selling price demanded (and received) for individual lithographic prints produced that year. They brought sixty dollars per copy, contrasting dramatically with earlier prices of fifteen dollars or even ten dollars.

The death of Jay Hambidge in March was both a shock and a personal loss to the artist, who had been his most active and vocal protagonist in the United States. He unhesitatingly agreed to the request from Hambidge's widow that he try to put her late husband's papers sufficiently in order to make possible the production of a book—but he soon appreciated his shortcomings as an editor and turned the task over to others more competent in the field.

In early spring, he painted *Riverfront*, the last New York scene to come from his brush. After a fortnight of jury duty, he returned to his studio in Nineteenth Street to create *Picnic*, a mysteriously idyllic and romantic picture that reminds us greatly of the feeling he conveyed in *The White Horse* of about eighteen months before.

There was one minor aggravation in the first week of May. *Collier's* had purchased from George a drawing called *Ringside*, which was reproduced in the current issue in a form so cut and trimmed that the artist believed the work (and, by extension, he himself) had been defamed. He wrote the editors a letter in which he offered to sue them for libel—one of the first instances of an artist claiming that a faulty or altered reproduction of his work constituted libel. The reply he received was at once apologetic and evasive. This so infuriated Bellows that he instructed his lawyer to institute proceedings against *Collier's* at once. Even in those good old days, however, when one might expect to learn the outcome of a civil court action during one's own lifetime, there was delay involved.

After the intense activity and emotional drain of the

winter and spring, the prospect of an easygoing summer at Woodstock seemed more welcome than usual. The season in the mountains began auspiciously. Soon after their arrival there, the Bellowses and Storys exchanged congratulations on learning that George's lawyer had won the first and most important round in his legal fight with *Collier's;* it was his attorney's conviction that having established the principle that a picture could in fact be libeled, a thought he had at first considered novel and implausible, the initial decision would be sustained on appeal—as it eventually was.

George occupied himself in the ways that gave him the most pleasure. He indulged in the usual variety of sports, especially tennis. And he painted. Of the pictures accomplished during this final stay at Woodstock, none is more touching than the portrait of his younger daughter in a long, striped dress—to which he gave the title *Lady Jean.*

In August, he began to have sharp pains in the abdomen. For a time he accepted Emma's counsel that the source of the trouble lay in his mind, his spirit, not in his flesh; many devoted athletes seem to enjoy pain as evidence of their exertions. But when the pangs came more frequently and were less bearable, he consulted Woodstock's general practitioner, who told him that he was suffering from an inflamed appendix and that he should lose no time in seeing to an appendectomy.

George Bellows, the man of iron, chose to ignore the doctor's advice—though he was unable to ignore the pains, which were particularly acute when he engaged in physical activity. He cut down on sports, and pretended to cut down on his smoking—which simply meant that when he wanted a cigarette, he left the house, something he did very frequently. He professed to feel better.

When the Storys took the Bellows children back to New York for the opening of school, George gave himself up entirely to painting—*Nude on a Hexagon Quilt* (which, to Emma's curious dismay, he had originally given the title of *Venus*), *Mr. and Mrs. Philip Wase* (a local Woodstock couple whose features are portrayed in a manner suggestive of the work of Grant Wood a decade later), *Two Women* (based on Titian's painting *Sacred and Profane Love*), and three paintings of the Catskill country scene; *Risley's Barn, Jim Twadell's Place,* and *My House, Woodstock.*

Before departing from Woodstock, the artist arranged for a local carpenter to come down to the city the following month to put down a new floor in his studio; after nearly fourteen years of abuse, it required replacement. On reaching New York, still feeling an occasional twinge in the region of his appendix, he tried to resume his active life, and for a time he succeeded. He prepared forty-two paintings to be sent to Chicago for an important exhibition, and helped to make plans with the director of the local branch of Durand-Ruel, a major international art concern, for a one-man show the next year.

Fortunately, perhaps (for it would have been too much for him), he could do no lithography that fall, because Bolton Brown was suffering from rheumatism and was unable to operate the press. To add to the gloom of Brown's ailment and his own came word of Aunt Fanny Daggett's death, in November. George wrote of the old lady: ". . . It gave me a great sensation . . . to have her bring me on her visits some drawings which I had made as a little boy . . . , the earliest evidence of my tendencies to be an artist."

While he was working on what was to be his last large oil, *Jean, Anne and Joseph,* Bellows began to call in from gallery owners all over the country the paintings of his that they had been holding on consignment. The pains in his abdomen must have been worse than they had been in the summer—though he made no mention of them to Emma. He may have been trying to pay no attention to them himself, yet this attempt to put some of his complicated business affairs in order certainly suggests that he recognized that he was ill, possibly very ill.

In December, Howard Monett wrote his uncle to say that Laura, the artist's half sister, was dying in Columbus. Under normal circumstances, Bellows would have made the journey to Ohio, but he just didn't feel up to it. Laura Monett died shortly before Christmas, thus leaving George the last member of his own Bellows generation, and ending a family connection that stretched back for almost a century, to his father's birth in 1827, in an American past that seemed impossibly remote.

The pain was now so incessant that Bellows had almost learned how to come to terms with it, to ignore it. He and Emma attended an early performance of Eugene O'Neill's new play, *Desire Under the Elms*. While the long drama depressed him terribly, the more so in his present state, he was also deeply stirred by it, and expressed a wish to portray the playwright from New London who had once shared the big studio at 1947 Broadway almost two decades before. He was not to have this wish granted.

On December 20, George completed the last picture he ever painted, *The Picket Fence*, which he had begun at Woodstock the previous summer. It was very much in the style of the little rural scenes he had been working on in September. It is tempting, now, to read an exceptional feeling of loneliness into this little picture, but in almost every Bellows seascape, landscape, and urban scene there is a pervasive loneliness; and art is, for the most part, lonely employment.

George and Emma celebrated New Year's Eve with Robert and Marjorie Henri, joined by only a handful of

close friends—Will and Effie Glackens, and Gene and Elsie
Speicher. The talk was cheerful, centering mainly on the
opening of the New Society's third exhibition, which was to
take place only a few days thence.

The next morning, the painter refused to take any nour-
ishment. He attributed his lack of appetite to overindul-
gence the night before. Emma knew better and understood
that her husband was very unwell, but her religious scruples
prevented her from summoning a physician. The morning
after, George decided that he would begin to replace the
floor of his studio by himself, since the carpenter from
Woodstock had failed to appear as promised. While he
was working, he suddenly doubled over in pain, and cried
out for Emma. Discarding all her reservations, personal and
religious, she immediately called a doctor, who ordered
the painter to be transported at once to Post Graduate
Hospital, barely two blocks from the Bellows house in
Nineteenth Street. There he underwent emergency surgery.
The physician in Woodstock had made a perfectly accurate
diagnosis; George's appendix required removal. The operation was a success, but the patient's condition was so run-
down after months of obstinate endurance that his recovery
from the shock of surgery was not at all certain. Emma
spent the next three days and nights at her husband's side;
during much of the time, if he was conscious at all, George
was delirious.

On January 5, Emma Bellows tore herself from the bed-
side long enough to put in an appearance at the opening
of the New Society exhibition. No one who didn't know
that George was lying in a state of semi-consciousness in
a hospital bed would have guessed it from his wife's
demeanor of utter tranquillity. If she herself sensed that
her husband was going to die, she refused, by an act of
absolute faith, to allow herself to believe it. She returned

directly from the gallery to the hospital, leaving George only occasionally for a few hours of fitful sleep. It was early in the morning of January 8 that she received a phone call from the hospital to announce that George Bellows had succumbed a few moments before.

If it had been impossible for Emma Bellows to believe that her husband was dying, it was equally impossible for her to believe that he was dead. Many ignorant outsiders accused the miserable widow of being responsible, because of her faith in Christian Science, for the long postponement of surgery that the Woodstock physician had so urgently prescribed. In fact, as we have noted, Emma had nothing to do with this delay. George Bellows was dead because he was convinced, like many other people, that if he just waited long enough, the pain would go away.

Yet poor Emma had no need for the blame of others. She blamed herself for not having compelled George to consult a doctor in New York. In her anguish and grief following his death, she turned all arrangements for a funeral over to friends. The result was a ceremony that the painter himself would have been appalled by—a solemn service in the Neo-Gothic nave of the Church of the Ascension, on Fifth Avenue at Tenth Street. The pallbearers were mainly members of "The Eight"—Henri, Sloan, Glackens, Maurice Prendergast, and Ernest Lawson; the single exception was Eugene Speicher.

Many important artists and collectors were in attendance. Perhaps the most incongruous figure there was Charles Dana Gibson, whose work had provided Bellows with his very first inspiration more than thirty years before. Gibson was President of the National Academy of Design and therefore present in his official capacity; though he certainly wasn't an invariable admirer of George's work (his praise for *The Enemy Arrive* notwithstanding), he couldn't help being an admirer of the man. This might well have been George's epitaph: "He left no enemies, because he made no enemies." Of almost no man, regardless of his calling, can so very much be said.

Afterword

It is usual for the reputation of an artist to enjoy an almost indecently meteoric ascent immediately after his demise. It had seemed, just before George's death, that he had achieved in life so high a place that there was no direction for *his* reputation to go except downward. But the "usual" enhancement of a man's name was not a description of the reaction to George Bellows' death. Hyperbole was beggared in editorials from every paper in the city. It was an astounding response, and one for which there is no ready explanation.

It may have been his comparative youth; he wasn't even halfway through his forty-third year of life. It was certainly not that he was a major public figure; his features were known to few. He was the most popular painter of his day, but not until the death, thirty-one years later, of Jackson Pollock at about the same age, was there such an orgy of praise in the public prints. Pollock, however, had been a revolutionary artistic figure; George Bellows had simply been a nice man and a good painter.

Emma Bellows comported herself with as much dignity during the first year of her widowhood as she had shown in the few days of his final illness. She saw to it that the Durand-Ruel show took place as scheduled, and was gratified, without seeming the least overwhelmed, when the directors of the Metropolitan Museum of Art requested her permission to organize a large-scale retrospective exhibition of George's work for the autumn of 1925. He was by far the youngest artist ever to be recognized in this way by that institution.

George Bellows' legacy to his wife and children was larger than anyone would have imagined—more than six hundred finished paintings and literally thousands of drawings and lithographic prints. In 1925 alone, Emma disposed of sixty thousand dollars worth of her late husband's work, three times as much as he had realized in his most prosperous year. From his death until her own, in 1959, his widow managed both his estate and his public memory with exemplary intelligence and taste.

Bellows' work has gradually entered every major American collection, public and private. And this is just as it should be. For the solid basis of his work (like his qualities as a man) rests on his nativity; he was completely an American product both in his manner of painting and the matter he elected to paint. Critics have conjectured at boring length about the kind of artist he might have become had he lived out his normal span. We must content ourselves with the George Bellows who really was—and that is enough: a kindly friend, a skilled painter, a concerned citizen.

INDEX

Donald Braider grew up in New York City and Cooperstown, New York. He studied at Swarthmore College, and during World War II the Army sent him to Grenoble, and later to Oxford. Braider's great interest has always been art. He wrote PUTNAM'S GUIDE TO THE GREAT ART CITIES OF EUROPE. Before that, he wrote a novel inspired by the death of Jackson Pollock, a close friend, titled THE PALACE GUARD, published by Viking. His COLOR FROM A LIGHT WITHIN, a fictionalized biography of El Greco, was a Reader's Digest Book Club selection. His most recent books are RAGE IN SILENCE, the story of Goya, and AN EPIC JOY, a novel about Rubens. Mr. Braider is now Assistant to the Headmaster of the Wooster School in Danbury, Connecticut, where he taught French for six years.